Alex Henshaw

Alex Henshaw grew up in the Twenties and Thirties, and his first aircraft was a Gipsy I Moth. He set his heart on winning the King's Cup Air Race, which he achieved after years of practice and scientific experimentation in 1938. In February 1939 he broke all records to Cape Town and back in a modified Mew Gull. It was because of this peacetime experience that he was asked to join Vickers-Armstrong as a test pilot when war broke out. Now semi-retired from a business career, he is occupied in writing memoirs of racing, test-flying, record-breaking and world travel over a period of fifty years.

Alex Henshaw was awarded the MBE for war services, and the Queen's Commendation for bravery for saving life in the 1953 sea floods.

Sigh For A Merlin
Testing the Spitfire

Alex Henshaw

Arrow Books Limited
20 Vauxhall Bridge Road, London SW1V 2SA

An imprint of Random Century Group

London Melbourne Sydney Auckland Johannesburg and
agencies throughout the world

First published in Great Britain by John Murray 1979
Hamlyn Paperbacks edition 1980
Reprinted 1981 (twice) and 1984
Arrow edition 1986
Reprinted 1987 and 1990

Printed and bound in Great Britain by Cox & Wyman Ltd,
Reading

ISBN 0 09 948130 8

✳ *Contents*

	Illustration Sources	vii
	Sigh for a Merlin	xi
1	The storm breaks	3
2	Slow days at Weybridge	12
3	Spitfire and Walrus	22
4	Chief Pilot, Castle Bromwich	37
5	Showing off the Spitfire	50
6	Bother, bombs and a balloon	62
7	A Tomtit in the garden	75
8	Mr Churchill comes to see	89
9	Requiem for a Tomtit	104
10	Skewgear and prop	123
11	A son gained, a boot lost	144
12	Rolling the Lanc	155
13	Dinghy on the loose	167
14	Two of the very best	181
15	Task completed	199
	Epilogue	203
	Summary of flying from Castle Bromwich	205
	Index	207

Illustration Sources

The Author and Publisher warmly thank all those who helped during the picture research for this book: in particular, for his continual encouragement and advice, Mr Hugh Scrope of Vickers-Armstrong Ltd. Vickers-Armstrong supplied the following photographs in the insert: page 1, top, left and right; page 2, top and bottom; page 3, top; page 5, top and bottom. The other photographs are from the Author's personal collection. Mrs Dorothy Couzens drew the maps.

Sigh For A Merlin

✳ Sigh for a Merlin

This is the tale of a thoroughbred. A thoroughbred with which I lived, almost day and night, for over five years during World War II: the Supermarine Spitfire.

It is universally accepted that the Supermarine Spitfire with its perfect artistic symmetry and unique design was conceived by the remarkable but tragic R. J. Mitchell. On Mitchell's early death this embryo was left to be developed by a small but highly experienced and competent team with which he had long been associated. It is my regret that time, space and opportunity have not permitted me to pay due tribute to every one of these comparatively unknown team members who, with their own particular expertise, played such an important part in the development of the Spitfire: naturally enough, the focal point of my story must be the flying in which I was involved. Mutt Summers had the privilege of being the first to fly the original prototype, but from then on Jeffrey Quill was to have control of the development test programme that with the full-time support of the Supermarine design team, first at Woolston and then later at Hursley Park, was to continue from 1936 until the end of World War II. It is impossible to evaluate each individual's contribution to the sustained success in design and performance of the Spitfire over the years but I am quite sure of one thing: no one that I know could have made a greater impact with such balanced judgement and flying ability in the meticulous field of test-flying a fighter aircraft than Jeffrey Quill.

Jeffrey was a young officer of 23 when he left the RAF to test and develop Spitfires of the first contract given to Supermarines at Southampton. He had already proved his calibre in many ways, including a period in the RAF Met. Flight. Flying each single day was expected and with the limited navigational aids available at that time, a return to a fog-bound base was not the easy routine exercise it would be today. He also had a very intelligent understanding of technical problems and could expound his views and theories in an articulate and lucid manner; this, coupled with his outstanding airmanship and his professional integrity, put him in a class which in my experience was rare indeed. Although not required or expected of him, Jeffrey insisted on familiarisation with every aspect of his work: participation in the Battle of Britain and operations at sea with the Fleet Air Arm were to him a means of perfecting his knowledge and comprehension, vital for the production of a proficient weapon of war.

Our paths did not actually cross until the outbreak of war. When they did I gained two things beyond price, my experience and love of the Spitfire and a friendship and respect that has not altered or weakened over 40 years.

The same age as Jeffrey, I was at the identical time as his early work on the Spitfire involved with another aircraft that was to become famous: the Percival Mew Gull. In July 1938, after six years of air racing experience in a variety of machines, came for me the triumphant climax: victory in the King's Cup Air Race in a modified Mew Gull, G-AEXF, at the fastest speed ever. Few know the effort, the cost and the anxiety that went into preparing the Mew Gull for this British Blue Riband event. Seven months later, in the same machine after much further preparation and with a different engine, all records to Cape Town and back were broken. This story has never yet been told, although it still stands as a solo record to this day. Perhaps, sometime, I will get down to it and tell how a tiny racing machine crossed jungle and desert, day and night, without air or ground aids in the glorious, carefree days of peace just before the world erupted into war.

My story is not about war but of a weapon of war—one which probably had a greater impact on a people to survive and put more heart into their morale when at its lowest ebb, than anything ever created in modern times. At the same time that it sustained and encouraged every man, woman and child in a small island under attack, it struck not only a physical blast but a strange psychological terror into its opponents as they heard its name over the radio.

Associated with this remarkable machine from start to finish of over five years of bitter warfare at both ends of the globe will for ever be the equally famous engine, the Rolls-Royce Merlin. The name means different things to different people. Certainly to the fighters, the bombers, the Fleet Air Arm and so many other important wielders of war the sound of a Merlin engine meant supremacy in the air.

Although this is not a tale of the Merlin, there is a great deal here about it and there came a time when we had to choose a suitable title for the book. One day I happened to be chatting near my home with an RAF Wing Commander (retired) now dressed in dark grey slacks and Norfolk jacket. Suddenly out of the blue and on its way to Coningsby was a fighter of the Battle of Britain Flight right over our heads.

We both stopped talking and looked up—the crisp steady note of the old Merlin as joyous a sound as ever it was all those years ago. The ex-Wing Commander said absolutely nothing—then he sighed. It was such a poignant sigh. I felt it must have invoked so many memories of the days when the Wing Commander was young, daring and vigorous and like a Knight of the Crusade had leapt onto the Spitfire and its Merlin to ride into the pages of history.

The silence was still uninterrupted. Thoughts and memories began to flicker through my mind. I remembered crashing badly and the terrifying sound of things being torn apart; closing my eyes as the ruptured earth flung pieces of metal over my crouching head; the peculiar smell of oil, petrol and glycol and damp earth hanging in my nostrils. Then the panic as I struggled out of parachute, harness and shattered cockpit— and then the silence. An almost deathly silence. As I prayed a word of thanks over the crumpled wreckage and the large black mass buried in the soft ground—once a powerful, gleaming engine—I heard this sigh. It may have been a pressure-relief valve, or glycol, or oil on hot metal, but in the emotion of the moment it became a sound I shall always remember. What better epitaph to a wonderful machine and a magnificent engine than to call my book *Sigh for a Merlin*?

There are some gifts in life that are beyond price—although we are not always aware of them at the time. My wife Barbara was married under the rapid thud of heavy gunfire, the rat-tat-tat of machine-guns and the scream of aircraft diving. She has now walked beside me for nearly forty years—she more than anyone knows the sorrow, the pain and the frustration that has been part of our life; but she has also been there to receive the applause, the success and the rewards that have come our way. Our son Alex is the culmination of this wonderful partnership.

If any thanks are due for this small record of events which took place during the most crucial period in our history, then they are due to these two people. It is their love, loyalty, faith and confidence that has been responsible for the publication of my story.

ALEX HENSHAW

1 ✳ *The storm breaks*

I SUPPOSE every man beyond a certain age, when there is time for reflection over the past, is able to say 'That was the happiest or the greatest or the most memorable year of my life.' For me I think it was the spring of 1939.

After my February Cape records, all doors were open to me, but that was only part of it; at the age of 26 I had few illusions about fame. In nearly ten years of following the careers of many world-famous flyers I had found myself sympathising with most, disgusted with many and sincerely admiring but a few. To be top of the world is to stand on a crust so thin that it can be shattered by one false step. The more I saw of notoriety the more I realised how little was sincere. At the same time I longed to escape the world of people to the simple company of dogs and horses in the tranquillity of the countryside.

It was not easy. Huge piles of letters and telegrams arrived every day, bringing offers and invitations of every kind. At first it was good fun and an education in itself. Home and overseas broadcasts, luncheons, dinners, lectures, first nights, demonstrations, etc. It did, however, have lighter moments. One broadcast on the effect of mental and physical fitness on long-distance flying was to be recorded for later transmission to France, Germany and Switzerland. When we arrived at the studios we were greeted by an excitable little Frenchman with a high-pitched voice; he informed us proudly that he was the compère and that all was in readiness. Having perused the script and set the disc in motion for recording, he said hastily 'My voice is a little high and does not record too well, so I always carry a bottle of medicinal throatwash,' and with a flustered apology he took a long draught from a small flask. In the midst of the recording we were stopped by the engineer operating the disc as he was unable to balance the tone correctly. There was a short delay during which the compère had another gulp from his flask—and so it went on. The engineer stopped us several times and each time our friend would pull out his flask, bringing a grin and a wink from my father who was with me. There was obviously something stronger than throatwash in that flask, because after each swallow he became more excitable and his voice went a pitch higher until in the end he sounded like a soprano taking singing lessons. We laughed our way out of the studios and to this day each time I put on that record it sends us into fits of laughter.

But it all became too much. It was just impossible to be my normal self. I was beginning to feel like some film star, wearing a perpetual grin, having to be pleasant and thank and smile at all times. At the beginning of March Dad realised all this was getting me down so that I was drawn and edgy, and pushing all arguments to one side, he swept me off for a skiing holiday in Davos. The morning we arrived the sun shone with a startling brilliance on fresh fallen snow so tempting that we could scarcely wait to put our skis on. As always in Switzerland I found the way of life I loved. Refreshed and invigorated by the exercise and peaceful environment I felt much better by the time we had returned to England.

At this point Barbara seriously entered my world and as she is undoubtedly the greatest blessing in my life and plays such a key role in everything I do, I must introduce her.

One day in the winter of 1937 when I was working at Gravesend airfield on the new 'R' engine of the Mew Gull with Jack Cross of Essex Aero and his enthusiastic young racing team, I looked up to see a tall girl with fair hair in a tailor-made suit talking to some people outside the hangar. I felt an instant attraction towards her and asked Jack who she was. In a turmoil of feelings I heard him tell me she was Barbara Wenman, the daughter of a well-known sailing family, that she had just flown in from Paris and was due to return the next week to marry Guy de Chateaubrun, a flying friend of mine. I turned back to my work, but the memory of that glimpse stayed with me. I found it hard to analyse my feelings in the weeks that followed; we had never met, never spoken to each other, yet it was as if something was eating away at me inside. I had known a few girls but this was different.

A few months later Guy was killed testing an experimental aircraft at Coulommiers. It is not certain what really happened on that tragic day but Guy carried a parachute and in fact had previously baled out in an emergency from a Mew Gull. The fact that he did not do so on this occasion when the machine went into a straight dive created the assumption that he had been overcome by exhaust or petrol fumes. Like all his friends I was deeply shocked and upset by the tragedy, but I was in the thick of my Cape preparations and I forced myself to thrust it out of my mind. A short while later, in the hangar of Essex Aero I saw a light blue Vega Gull and asked Jack whose it was. With a leap in my heart I heard him say, 'The Countess de Chateaubrun's; she's going to sell it.' I thought Jack must hear the beating of my heart or notice my face, as I found myself saying, 'I think I had better handle this, I'm sure I can find her a buyer.' Once more, however, the pressures of the record attempt drove the matter from my mind.

Now, in March 1939, revived by the snows of Switzerland, I took my courage in both hands and telephoned the address in Meopham where Barbara's parents lived. She was in, would be pleased to discuss the Vega and would I come for tea.

I was greeted at the door by the most beautiful girl I had ever seen in my life and the feeling I had had in the hangar months before returned with a vengeance. I stayed as long as manners would permit after arranging to fly her Vega Gull up to my own hangar where it would be stored until sold. The next day I drove her up to London and a week later I asked her out to lunch before she returned to Paris. I don't remember what we had to eat, or whether I tasted anything, but I worked out that all I wanted to do was to be able to walk through life beside her. I knew that she was still suffering from the tragedy of the summer before but as I paused she looked at me, and I realised there was no need for any more words. When she left for Paris the next day I promised I would fly over as soon as I could get away.

I could not keep pace with all the commitments and invitations of that summer, but in July Dad and I did agree to go for the official opening of Elmdon airfield. We arrived in the Vega Gull, which was always kept in immaculate condition, but nevertheless I was a little surprised to be awarded a craftsman-designed artistic silver table ornament as the winner of the Concours d'Elegance for the best kept aircraft with the most interesting history. I was not to know that Elmdon aerodrome was to mean so much to me in the months to come or that I should be living in Hampton-in-Arden, a short distance away.

Earlier that year I had promised Bill Courtney, newspaper correspondent and publicity manager to various celebrities, to attend the Rolls-Royce official opening of Derby airfield. He had put a tremendous amount of publicity work into this and the aerodrome was packed with private, industrial and service personalities. One sensed about this time, however, that there were more serious undertones to the usual gaiety that generally prevailed at such meetings and I think we all eyed our latest military aircraft with more than casual interest; at the same time, when we saw our anti-aircraft defence units give a somewhat childish demonstration, we hoped to God they would be in better shape if and when the time came.

I received a very imposing and impressive looking card from Berlin inviting me once again to visit the Frankfurt International Air meeting. I accepted and we invited Flying Officer A. E. Clouston, whose record to the Cape and back in the de Havilland Comet I had recently broken in the Mew Gull G-AEXF, to go along as our guest. An odd incident had happened shortly before we received the invitation. Several Germans including Herr Gerbrecht had attended a flying meeting at Eastbourne and Dad, who knew Gerbrecht liked

Scotch whisky said, 'I will see that you have some of my special blend, when you come over to the Lympne meeting in September.' Gerbrecht replied, 'Why not bring it when you come over to Frankfurt, as I shall not be able to make Lympne this year.' Now, if he had left it at that, we should have thought nothing about it, but he then seemed a little confused and said, 'I mean, I shall try to come over to Lympne, but September is a busy month for me.' And he appeared unnecessarily embarrassed as he explained this to us.

Our eyes opened when we landed at Frankfurt that year. Accustomed as we were to the pomp and ceremony at German official functions, I was astonished to see Gerbrecht and many other Germans whom we had always considered as civilians now in the uniform of the German Luftwaffe. Gerbrecht, as he saluted us, tried to ease the embarrassment by joking that this was after all an official occasion. Whilst I received the same VIP treatment, it was now of a very formal character and the warm, casual friendliness was less apparent. This time I was asked to clear customs and immigration, which had been waived on previous occasions, and I was not very pleased when informed by the immigration officer that I must have a visa to enter Germany. I had known that recently the British government had imposed similar conditions on all Germans entering the UK, and this was of course in retaliation, but I was so well known in Europe at that time that often I had gone about without the required documents and there had never been the slightest difficulty. As I was arguing with the immigration officer, someone behind me said in good English, 'Can I be of any assistance? You're Alex Henshaw, I know; I'm Max Immelmann.' I said, 'That's a famous name in aviation, but surely Immelmann was killed in the Great War?' He said, 'Yes, but I'm a cousin of his.'

The visa trouble was soon sorted out, but I still had to go into the city to pick them up. I wished when I arrived there that I had not gone, for facing me in front of this large government building where there were police everywhere was a long queue of Jews trying to get exit permits. The plight of these poor people, some of them with complete families and little children was pathetic and their treatment by the officials and police made my blood boil.

I was racing the Vega the next day and bearing in mind the generous treatment offered to me the year before I soon found that things had changed somewhat in that short period. The course was a closed circuit with many electric pylons dotted around at intervals. I soon realised that I was not going to do very well but as the entry was made up of a very large international field I carried on making the best effort I could. I was mindful of the powerful electrical overhead cables, but evidently others were less so. Towards the end of the last lap, I saw a burst of smoke and flame: one of the competitors in a four-seater Messerschmitt Taifun disappeared as his aircraft disintegrated on hitting the top of the heavy electric steel pylon. The standard of the flying, to say the least, in many cases left much to be desired; one pilot racing a German machine over the airport caught his wingtip on the ground, buckled the wing and was lucky to survive the crash. I finished an unhappy sixth and I was not surprised when I landed to find the Germans had beaten competitors from all over the world and had gained first, second and third places. I hoped their victory felt less hollow to them than it did to me. The papers made no mention of the deaths of the four people in the accident, but were filled with praises of the overwhelming German victory.

That evening we went to the beer garden situated on the banks of the Rhine, where we were entertained by most of the top German aviators, such as Udet, Gerbrecht, Seidemann and many others. I found Immelmann forthright, interesting and easy to talk to. He guessed my own views and tried to talk himself out of any embarrassment, but I was in the mood not to pull any punches. During the long evening and in the course of the conversation I said, 'There is not going to be another Munich you know; if you go through the Polish corridor we shall be at war within days.'

'You are making too much of this,' he said. 'What is Poland? A land of peasants. In this day and age you cannot have a decadent country such as this holding up the might of the German nation.'

'The principle is still there, just as in 1914, when you did exactly the same thing over Belgium.'

He continued, 'In any case there will be no war. There will be meetings, there will be discussions, there will be agreements, but there will be no war.'

'I am as certain as I sit here that if you carry this situation by force as you did in Czechoslovakia my country will go to war,' I answered.

'You are quite wrong, of that I am also sure,' he replied. 'There will be no war. But if as you say your government make a declaration against us, we have six million men under arms and you already have enough trouble with the Irish.'

Clouston and I wandered around the aerodrome the next day before we returned. As we examined the Messerschmitt 109 fighters lined up on the aerodrome we agreed that they were going to be tough opponents to cross swords with and we sincerely hoped it would never come to that. I asked Dad if August of 1914 was like August of 1939. He said no, in that beautiful summer of 1914 no one expected or believed in war with Germany, but in any case if it came it would be a bit of a lark and the thing was to have some fun before it was all over. I certainly did not feel like that during those tense days as August drew to a close, nor I think did anyone else. I felt sick to death with Hitler making demands and trampling across the face of Europe. I felt ashamed of our actions at Munich and our betrayal of Czechoslovakia. I desperately wanted there to be peace but not at any price.

It was but a few weeks later when I was on my way to a meeting of farmers and fruitgrowers. The sun shone out of a clear blue sky and life seemed good as I drove down the dry, dusty roads. The summer was far from over; a cock-pheasant strutted across the narrow lane to lose itself in the long grass;

a noisy, colourful jay weaved low in front of the car to disappear between long rows of Bramleys on the left; Tony, my Labrador, stirred beside me and raised his ears. I knew the signal, chose a quiet grass gateway and let him out for a run—but I wasn't going to rush. It was too wonderful a day for speed and the hot, lazy sun was having an effect; I decided to wait for the radio news and let him forage around a bit longer.

Just as the BBC news commentator started speaking, Tony barked to be let into the car and I missed the opening announcement, but I was shaken out of my daydream by the first words I managed to hear '. . . at dawn this morning troops, guns and tanks of the German Forces crossed the Polish frontier preceded by a heavy bombing attack . . .'. A surge of emotions and racing thoughts put my mind in complete confusion; after all the developments of recent months I should have been mentally prepared, but somehow I had never really believed that a modern civilised power could stoop to such folly.

I sat quite still for a few moments, then as I started forcing myself to think out the immediate future, I turned the car round and headed back to Wisbech. A plan started forming; I would pick up my things in Wisbech, go on home, pick up the Vega Gull and fly straight out to Paris to bring Barbara back. Then I'd get into a fighter squadron as soon as I could.

I drove back with the radio on, expecting at any moment the declaration by England and France of war with Germany. It did not come. Instead there was a great deal of speculation and unsubstantiated reports from various observers in different parts of Europe. There were announcements by the British government and odd statements from Ministers but nothing dramatic. Then out of a welter of words a simple, plain statement stood out: 'All British civil and private aircraft are grounded until further notice.' It so shocked me that I almost stopped the car. Until that moment it had not occurred to me that events were going to change with such tumultuous speed— that the life to which we had become so accustomed was to be so deeply affected. It was like a slap in the face to realise that after seven years of flying where I liked and when I liked, in my own aircraft, I was no longer free as a bird; there was now no question of picking up Barbara in Paris and nonchalantly ferrying her home.

As I drove on many memories came together with a new significance; those strictly regimented groups of marching boys and girls Dad and I had seen on the banks of the Rhine as early as 1935; the pilots, Major Seidemann and Herr Gerbrecht wanting to be left very much to themselves on their tour of the British Isles; the flight of the *Hindenburg* over England; the bomb racks I had seen on the Junkers transports in 1936, locked in a hangar in Eastern Germany; the secret grass landing strips amongst the pine forests near Danzig. How blind we had been to the build-up of the Nazi war machine. Churchill had told the people—but who would listen? In days now would be in uniform and taking orders. My days as a celebrity were over.

2 ✳ *Slow days at Weybridge*

I HAD IN FACT overrated the Germans' military machine and their strategy. I had always felt that within hours of war, maybe even before, their hordes of bombers would be blasting every military objective in this country, and even with my comparatively limited knowledge, I knew they could do so almost unopposed. But the quick attack was never made.

After much trouble I had been able to reach Barbara in Paris on the phone, but she had already made plans and was leaving at once by train. Could I meet her at Victoria Station in the morning? Victoria Station was bedlam, but everyone was calm, polite and grimly cheerful as train after train came in and people strained at the barriers to see if they could pick out their loved ones. I waited all day without moving from the platform, watching the barrier exits and the brief information going up from time to time on a large blackboard. I eventually caught sight of Barbara as she stepped down from the train, looking like everyone else, very tired and weary.

We waited patiently for the Prime Minister's announcement. It was not immediately forthcoming, but even so every person was conscious it was inevitable. I told Dad of my intention to join the RAF right away and he advised caution: 'How do you know they'll put you in a fighter squadron?' he answered. 'Once you sign on that dotted line you could end up peeling potatoes.' On his shrewd advice I wrote to the Air Ministry offering my services in any active flying capacity. I got a very prompt reply stating that the matter would be given consideration. When I heard nothing further after a week I decided to do something about it myself and wrote to various friends in the aviation world. The most interesting reply came from Captain Wilfred Dancy, who was then resident Technical

Officer with Supermarine at Southampton. He said that the Spitfire contract had just been increased and that he had written to Vickers-Armstrongs Ltd, recommending me, and that an appointment could be arranged for me to meet Captain Summers, the Chief Test Pilot, at Weybridge and the General Manager, Mr Trevor Westbrook.

Before going to Weybridge, Barbara and I both had a few things to attend to in London and we were surprised to see so many already in uniform. Some of my friends were showing off their Service and rank very proudly, whilst others having been called up on the reserve from prestigious civilian jobs, were making excuses for their non-commissioned stripes. I was asked time and time again what I was going to do. Of course I could only say I hadn't made up my mind, but was searching around.

I waited in the reception lounge of Vickers-Armstrongs at Weybridge as they put out a call for Captain Summers. A few minutes later he arrived with Group Captain Webster, formerly of the 1929 Schneider Trophy team, who was now an RAF overseer at the Weybridge factory. I had not met him before but Dad had told me he was a good scout, as he had spent some time with him in Cairo during 1933. Mutt Summers was a burly, thickset individual, who spoke in a series of short sentences; I said that I was interested in the Spitfire project as explained to me by Wilf Dancy, if it was still available and if he thought I could hold the job down. He said I had better come along with him and see the General Manager, Trevor Westbrook. Westbrook was dynamic and so busy that I wondered he had time to do anything. When Summers tapped on his door Westbrook barked for us to come in and with two telephones on the go at the same time, he waved us to a couple of seats. When Westbrook had time to put the telephones down, Summers introduced me and Westbrook said, 'Why do you want to come to us?' I said that I was looking for something suitable as I was in the process of closing up and rearranging my own affairs so that I could do a war job where I was best

suited. 'What makes you think you will be any good to us?' he
barked. Before I could reply Mutt said, 'We've got the Wellington contract coming along, there's the development work on
the Vulture, Quill has his hands full with the Spitfire programme
and there is the Sea Otter development; we shall have to have
more pilots and we may as well get the best before other firms
collar them.' Westbrook gave me a fierce look and said. 'We
want pilots who can get aircraft up into the air and keep them
there. If you can do that you'll do fine, if not you're no use to
us.' He then pressed buttons, picked up the phone and the
interview was over. Mutt said as we left, 'Don't take too much
notice of Trevor, his barks are worse than his bite.' But I
guessed that Mutt did not think much of his manner: much
later I learned how much Westbrook achieved by his dynamism.

I was shown over the works, and given a brief explanation
of the type of flying I should carry out. I left promising I would
report for duty in fourteen days if I could clear my own affairs
in time.

Barbara and Dad were delighted, I think they had felt I
would rush into something I would regret and that at Weybridge they could at least visit me without difficulty. Leaving
home was a wrench; I knew I should miss everything, but I
never knew how much until later on. I couldn't take Tony
and he slunk around with his tail down aware that something
was on as I patted Ranger, Beauty, Spitfire and Quicksilver in
their stables and said goodbye to many things I had loved.

I think without question those weeks at Weybridge were the
unhappiest of my life, certainly the most miserable of my
flying experience. Mutt Summers tried to be kind and helpful
and he showed me around rather like a new exhibit; but we
had different personalities, the atmosphere at Weybridge was
one to which I was unaccustomed and worst of all I got no
pleasure or satisfaction out of the work, if one could call it that.
The only other pilot was Maurice Hare, an ex-naval officer,
quiet and placid with a charming wife, Margot, and two little
girls.

Mutt took me up in a Wellington and told me very casually what to do; this was the first time I had flown a large machine and operating from the bowl of Brooklands race track did nothing to inspire me and I suddenly felt that I had become very inadequate. Some aeroplanes, like a well tuned and balanced sports car, inspire me and in less than no time at all I feel at home and in control. The Wellington to me, was not like this. To start with, it was fitted with Bristol radial engines nearly ten times the power of those I had been accustomed to operate and the response felt very slow indeed. On a small aircraft engine with short throttle linkage connectors, the control response is almost immediate. On the Wellington I found as I opened the throttles there was a time lag before the engines responded and the same when closing down. This of course was only a matter of practice and I soon got the hang of it.

The take-off was also disappointing to me; with all that power and no load on board I expected the machine to bound forward and leap off the ground; instead it would waddle along on the rough airfield at Weybridge rather like a fat mallard.

In the air, it seemed to me at that time slow and cumbersome and had I not been anxious to gain twin-engine bomber experience I should have been very disappointed indeed. With the geodetic form of construction it was a very flexible machine and I was somewhat shaken to notice how much the wings deflected in bumpy conditions. It was, however, very safe and easy to fly and could be set down inside the Weybridge racing bowl almost like a Tiger Moth. I was to fly it with a variety of engines, including Merlins, but whilst I cannot say I really disliked the Wellington, I am afraid, unlike some much heavier machines I was to fly, I never really liked it.

I think had there been a heavy flying programme, I should probably quickly have found confidence and satisfaction, but as it was, flying was usually less than an hour each day, and my spirits sank lower and lower. I could not even justify my

existence with some tough bad-weather flying, as Hare said to
me one day when I had landed in moderate conditions, 'We
do not fly if we cannot see that church on the hill,' pointing to
a familiar landmark then obscured. The work also lost interest
when during my first development trials on one particular
project, I had made my notes in flight and had been making
mental observations as to how I would embrace these in my
flight report to the design office. That evening the chief
inspector came up to me and said, 'I've made your report out
for you chief, if you'll sign it.' I could tell this was the normal
practice, so I signed and thanked him for the excellence of his
work, which I had to admit was probably far better than I
could have written it; but at the time it left me very empty. I
was also not used to the intrigue and petty jealousy that went
on around the works and to me it seemed the height of hypocrisy
to drink and be extremely friendly with a person and then
scheme and plot against him when his back was turned. Also I
hated wasting time and this we did day after day. I would go
out to the pilots' hut on the airstrip and ask what the flying
programme was for the day; if told there might be a job later
on, I hung around until Hare or Summers arrived and then we
would all go over to the Brooklands club, in which pre-war I
had had some very pleasant times, and have a drink. Here
Hare and Summers would play dice and I would talk to John
Cobb, the water speed record holder, who was usually there,
or with some other member, until lunchtime; then we would
stroll back to the factory across the airstrip for a meal.

Westbrook must have realised the little amount of work
three pilots were doing and one morning Mutt came to me and
said, 'Westbrook thinks it would be a good idea if you did
some work in the main office when not flying to familiarise
yourself with other aspects of aircraft production; I am to take
you to B. A. Duncan's office.' And then out of the side of his
mouth with a grin he said, 'This is one of Trevor's whims.
Don't take too much notice of it, just show your face occasionally to Duncan and say you're busy flying.'

At the time I welcomed the idea and was willing to do anything. Duncan was a hardworking, dry, silent man; I certainly did my best at any job he gave me but we never really got on. I was a little taken aback when he said, pointing to a little typist's desk in the corner of his not very large office, that I could use that; handing me a pile of books and records, he told me to trace every Wellington in each squadron and at all maintenance units and list the number of modifications still outstanding on each machine. I set to work with a will, but could not help reflecting that many of my friends would laugh if they saw me doing what after all was simply a junior clerk's job. I was further embarrassed when the main office block soon knew who was in Duncan's department and were making excuses to enter Duncan's office and observe the new exhibit.

I religiously worked in Duncan's office when not flying, but one day he told me to go into the factory and find the Stock Control Manager and ask him why certain spares had not been dispatched. I did not know my way around the factory very well and had some difficulty locating this man; when I did so he was very busy dealing with a number of men trotting around rather like a pack of hounds. I politely waited a suitable opportunity and stepping forward said, 'Mr Duncan would like to know why spares have not been dispatched to Hull-avington.' He looked at me, assumed I was Duncan's office boy, and said sharply: 'I deal with spares dispatch as best I can, and you go back and tell Duncan I don't want any of his bloody office boys chasing me around; and if he is not satisfied, to climb off that pedestal of his and come down and see me himself.' I had a list of spares in my hand and as I trembled with rage, as calmly as I could I slowly and deliberately tore the list of spare parts into small pieces and flung them into the face of the manager saying, 'I'm not Duncan's office boy and if you want to know what you and Duncan can do with your spares, I'll bloody soon tell you.' The sight of his face and the men around him should have made me laugh as I stormed out, but I was so wild I couldn't wait to reach Duncan and get the matter off my chest. I flung open Duncan's office door but he was out at a production meeting, so I went to the main office used by Mutt and Maurice, to cool off; fortunately neither of them was there. (The sequel was to take place a month later, when I had to drop into Weybridge with a Spitfire to pick up some spares for Eastleigh. I had previously telephoned Tommy Gammon, the Works Manager, and he was waiting in the car with the spares as I landed. To my amusement, with him in the car was the head of the department I had had the words with over the spare parts for Duncan; I could see from the look on his face that Tommy had been singing my praises and the last person he expected to see was Duncan's late 'office boy'. He didn't know what to do with himself and was covered with confusion but I smiled at him and said, 'Haven't we met before?' He blushed and said, 'I'm terribly sorry, sir, but I didn't know; Duncan's always sending someone around to do his chasing and I thought you were one of his office crowd.')

I stamped into the pilots' office and slumped into the large chair. The telephone rang soon afterwards and the operator said, 'Mr Sidney Cotton for Mr Alex Henshaw.' After we had exchanged the usual courtesies he said, 'Could you have dinner with me tonight at the Royal Air Force club; I have a proposition, which I think might interest you.' I hadn't seen Cotton for some months. Sid Cotton was an adventurer but a very able one and as Tommy Rose once said to me, 'You never know with Sid, he's either a multi-millionaire or flat broke.' His name of course will always be associated with the old 'Sidcot' flying suit.

When I arrived at the RAF club that evening, Sid put an astonishing proposal to me and at that moment it seemed a heaven-sent opportunity. The RAF had been trying to get good photographs of the German defences without much success; Cotton had arranged an appointment with Sir Kingsley Wood, the Secretary of State for Air, and as he walked into his office he laid a marvellous selection of extremely good photographs of the Siegfried Line in front of him. As he told me this story he showed me the same photographs. As I looked at them I saw the exact picture I had seen through a gap in the clouds over the German frontier when we crossed there, quite contrary to the regulations, on our way to Frankfurt. I blurted out, 'Why you cunning devil, Sid, you didn't take those photographs recently! They were taken last summer on our way to Frankfurt. I reckon you flew the same course as we did, without diverting to Liège as we were instructed.' He grinned and said, 'Well there's no need to tell the Minister that, is there?' He then went on that as a result of this first fortuitous meeting with the Air Minister, he had been given *carte blanche* to form his own operations unit. The idea was to collect a small select team of competent pilots and in consultation with political and service chiefs to send them into enemy territory to photograph highly strategic targets. On their return they would wait for adverse weather conditions to evade the German defence screen and then go in to bomb the targets out of existence. He went on that he had the power to requisition any aircraft that would be suitable for bombing and photography, and had in fact already started to build up his unit at Heston. As proof of his authority he said he had arranged recently for the British Navy to intercept a Dutch boat carrying American engines to Holland as he needed them badly.

'Where do I fit into this picture?'

'I want you to take charge of flying operations.'

The idea appealed to me, but as I had never been in the RAF I could see lots of problems with red tape; he had already gone into this and any minor difficulties had already been ironed out. I said I would let him know after the weekend, but in my own mind I knew this was the job I had waited for and that the answer would be yes.

It was late when I returned to Weybridge. Next morning I was up and about early as I had a test to carry out on one of the Wellington magnetic-mine machines. Magnetic mines were being laid in the Thames estuary and elsewhere and they had taken a heavy toll of our shipping in the early stages of the war.

Rex Pierson, the Chief Designer at the Weybridge works, and George Edwards with others had devised what looked like an enormous halo round the Wellington; this halo was energised by a 200-h.p. Gipsy engine placed in the fuselage of the Wellington and when flown over the magnetic mines at low altitude, it exploded them. The test was very basic and did not take long, but it was about ten o'clock when I strolled into Duncan's office, a little calmer than I had been the day before. He grunted a greeting and stared pointedly at the clock. I paused and then said quietly, 'Duncan, I'm not your office boy, neither am I your messenger and just to keep the record straight I have not just wandered in here from my bed, but have in fact been flying since eight o'clock. From now on you had better get someone else to run your errands.' Duncan was so speechless that I had left the office before he had time to say a word; in fact I was not to see him again until I flew the first production Wellingtons at the Chester works some months later, after he had been appointed General Manager.

I went back to the pilots' office to think things over. I would tell Mutt that morning that I was leaving, meet Barbara later and tell her what I intended and then see Dad at the weekend. I was deep in thought as the door opened quietly and a trim dark-looking boy in black flying overalls, carrying a helmet and test pad, walked in. 'Hello,' he said, 'you must be Alex Henshaw. I'm Jeffrey Quill.' I liked him at once and was soon telling him how fed up I was kicking my heels around there. He said, 'That's ridiculous. You must come to us; we've got more work that we can cope with.' He then told me of the experimental work on the Spitfire, the sea trials in the Solent and the Channel with the Walrus and the development work on the new Sea Otter, so that I regretted very much I had not seen him when I first arrived at Weybridge. We parted with Jeffrey saying, 'We'd love to have you at any time if you would like to come.' I discussed my plans with Barbara and Dad. Both were dead set against me going to Sid Cotton; Barbara because we would be parted and Dad because he did not like the idea of me going into uniform. As he logically said, 'What happens if the scheme folds up? You're in the Air Force and there you'll have to stay; you could end up flying Tiger Moths—or, knowing what you are, more probably in the glass house.' The outcome was I promised to give Supermarines a trial before committing myself to Cotton.

Leaving Weybridge was not as simple as I thought. Summers tried to persuade me that anyone could fly fighters, but the real work was to fly and develop bombers, and that there were immense opportunities just around the corner. To be fair, however, when he saw my mind was made up he said, 'OK, but you'll have to see Westbrook first.' When I walked into Westbrook's office he barked, 'Well Henshaw, what do you want?' and tried to persuade me that there was plenty of work to do at Weybridge. When I disagreed and told him the aircraft were never available before eleven he called in his staff and bawled them out. It was acutely embarrassing. I said I was sorry I did not mean to cause any trouble but I still wanted to go to Supermarines and frankly if that were not possible I should have to hand in my resignation. 'Oh well,' he said somewhat subdued, 'if you feel that way about it, I suppose you had better go to Supermarines.' I found Mutt and told him. He said, 'You'd better report to George Pickering, he'll show you the ropes. Let me know how you get on as there is still a place for you here.'

It was the seventh of November, my birthday. I was 27 years old. As I drove down from Weybridge to Southampton I wondered if I was doing the right thing. It was a strange war, quite unlike anything I had expected. We had dropped a few leaflets on Germany; they had sunk some of our ships; we suffered a great deal of discomfort in the blackout. But otherwise life seemed to go on with no one unduly worried about the future, or so it seemed to me.

3 ✳ Spitfire and Walrus

I REPORTED to Eastleigh aerodrome, where I met George Pickering for the first time. I liked George tremendously. He was about eight to ten years older than Jeffrey and me. I don't think he really took test flying seriously although he was a very good pilot; but as he said himself his ambition was not to be the best pilot, but to live to be the oldest. I found Supermarines very different from Weybridge. To start with it was on a smaller scale and less affluent and ostentatious in its general mode of work and most of the operatives were ordinary people who had been in amphibious aviation for a long time and were dedicated to their work. I loved the conditions, got on well, I think, with everyone, and certainly did my utmost to do a good job. The district was also different from Weybridge; no smart clubs, away from the rich London commuters, so that at least I did not have to worry about the endless invitations to cocktail parties and other social gatherings.

I stayed at the Polygon hotel and the first night I stumbled out of the blackout to be almost blinded by the bright lights as I stepped into the hotel entrance. Blinking I heard someone say, 'My God, Alex Henshaw! What are you doing here, have you come to join us?' I then saw the room was full of Fleet Air Arm uniforms, worn by dozens of pilots I had known as civilians. The one who had shouted across to me was Henry Deterding and as he shook hands I was quickly joined by Ken Whittome, Bob Everett of Grand National fame, Jimmy Gardner, Guy Robson, Giles Guthrie and at the back I saw Laurence Olivier and Ralph Richardson. They had all joined up at the outbreak of war and were stationed at Eastleigh. We were to have some very pleasant times together during the next few weeks.

I was out early next morning and was the first to arrive at our little office on Eastleigh aerodrome. I had been thinking about flying my first Spitfire most of the night and sincerely hoped that I should not make a hash of it. As I had nothing else to do, I strolled the hundred yards or so along the final assembly block. Arthur Nelson, whom I had met the day before, was in charge and I asked him if he would mind if I sat in a fully assembled Spitfire to familiarise myself with the instruments and controls and in particular the rather clumsy chassis retraction gear. He replied, 'I'll do better than that; you can nip into this machine on the test-rig. There you can operate the flaps and lower and lift the wheels to your heart's content.' I was very glad of this offer. Although the cockpit was quite simple and straightforward, the chassis hydraulic pump handle was the same as one would see in the local garage to operate small jacks, except that the control handle in the Spitfire was big and solid and rather reminded me of the tiller on some sailing boats that did not use a wheel. It required quite an effort to operate the pump and I saw immediately that you had to change hands from the throttle and the control column to pump after take-off. Nelson put me on my guard when he laughingly said, 'Bet you a £1 you do a corkscrew the first time you go up.'

When I returned to the flight office Jeffrey suggested that I took one of the machines that were normally used for development work so that I could get to know the district—areas of which were heavily guarded and defended with multiple balloons and their lethal cables—and also to get the feel of the machine. He walked out with me to the tarmac and I studied the incomparable lines profiled against the dark hangars. I had exactly the same feeling as when I first flew the Mew Gull from the narrow strip at Luton. I felt a close affinity with this wonderful piece of machinery but at the same time, as at Luton, I wondered if I could measure up to the job. Jeffrey helped me on with my chute and pulled the straps of the Mae West tight, with a jocular remark. I wrote the aircraft number on the new

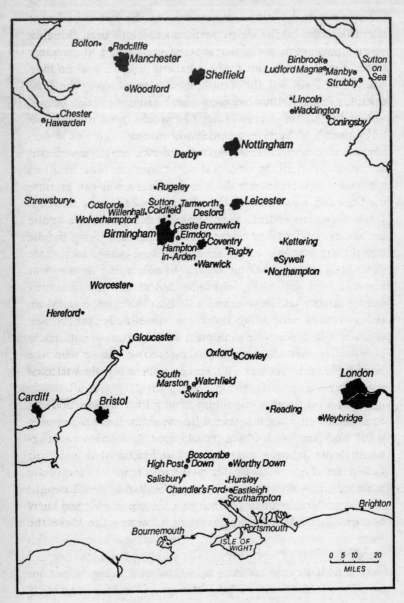

Principal airfields mentioned in the book

knee-pad Arthur Nelson had made for me, K9793, and climbed into the cockpit. My visit to the final assembly block did much to give me confidence so that I wasted no time in starting up.

As I taxied slowly out to the northern boundary of the grass field I had time to think of the technical details concerning the machine in which I was about to fly. It was a Mark I fitted with a Merlin III engine giving 980 hp at a pressure height of 1013·5 mm and 1000 hp at 15,000 ft, although this would vary slightly with temperature and forward ram effect through the air intake at speed. It carried less fuel than my Mew Gull: 84 gallons of 87-octane petrol. I had a take-off boost pressure controlled automatically to a maximum of 6 lb psi. It would achieve the remarkable speed of 365 mph* at 17,000 ft and could climb to almost 20,000 ft in ten minutes. The aircraft rolled comfortably over the grass, easy to control and not too difficult to see out of if you zig-zagged slowly so that your side views took in the whole field. The undercarriage was a little narrow so care had to be taken with sharp turns on the ground.

I was now ready to go. With the three-bladed metal two-position V/P airscrew in fine pitch I opened up slowly. I was over cautious with the machine and it took-off on its own in a ridiculously easy manner. Remembering Nelson's bet I selected the undercarriage up and pumped. I kept the aircraft steady but am not sure that without his warning I would have done so. In my concentration, however, I had overshot Jeffrey's warning point and saw that I was nearly over Southampton. Fortunately the balloons were down. The Spitfire flew as it had looked on the ground—a sheer dream; controls beautifully harmonised; positive and quick response; like a true thoroughbred, not a vice in the whole machine. I felt part of it and knew at once that I would give everything I possessed to make the

* Later in this account I use IAS to represent the speed shown on the airspeed indicator. Readers might like to be reminded of two things: first, that in a Walrus, Seafire or any other naval aircraft the speed is calibrated in knots; second that considerable under-reading of the true airspeed is caused by changes in temperature and altitude and sometimes position error. For instance, at 40,000 ft 200 IAS may represent a true airspeed of around 400 mph.

combination successful. I carefully swung round and put the
Spitfire into final approach, lowering the chassis, the flaps and
pulling back the sliding hood as I flattened out for the landing.
In my anxiety to complete a perfect landing and aware that I
had never previously stalled the machine I came in much too
fast. The 'float-off' seemed to go on for so long that instead
of the immaculate three-pointer I had intended, I finished
with the main wheels touching first and the tail gently afterwards.

George Pickering did most of the Walrus and Sea Otter work
and Jeffrey Quill was responsible for the Spitfire contract and
development programme. I found Jeffrey's approach to the job
somewhat different from that I had experienced at Weybridge:
meticulous, painstaking, calculated and reasoned, so that every
programme was discussed, analysed and flown to a pre-
determined pattern. This suited me and I enjoyed the discussions and work with Jeffrey as much as I disliked my period
at Weybridge. We worked closely and constantly and when
carrying out trials in rough water with the Walrus, we were
very often flying together. In all that time I think we only had
a few harsh words once, and that was all rather childish. As I
recall it the weather was bad and Jeffrey and I both had a
production test on a Spitfire to complete. I had made two trips
to check the flight trim and as I took off for the third time I
saw Jeffrey landing and thought he was going to do the same;
the cloud base was ten-tenths, heavy and very low and I was
anxious to put up a good show and complete the test if possible,
but I knew I must take care when I climbed up to check the
rated altitude at 15,000 ft and get in the dive. I kept below
cloud and in the pouring rain I flew out to our normal test
area in the Solent. I checked my bearings carefully between
Portsmouth and the Isle of Wight, which disappeared into the
cloud, and commenced my climb over the sea. Everything
went well; I dived out of the cloud almost exactly where I
expected and carefully weaved my way back to Eastleigh,
pleased with myself that I had been able to complete the test

and could hand the machine over to Len Levy, the Flight Shed Superintendent. When I returned to the pilots' office Jeffrey was sitting at his desk and I realised something was eating him; as soon as I walked in, he said, 'Don't you think you were taking a chance flying in that stuff?' I said I didn't think much of it, but I certainly didn't take any chances. 'Well,' he continued, 'I was flying and packed it up because I thought it was bloody unsafe.' 'Are you trying to tell me I shouldn't fly because you didn't?' I snapped, getting angry. No more words were said and we both sat in silence. George Pickering came in a little later and sensed the atmosphere at once: 'You know I ought to tan the backsides off both you boys, flying in this stuff; you wait until you get an old man like me, you'll learn more sense. Why as I drove in the gate even the bloody birds were walking.' We all burst out laughing at that and the incident was over.

My first job was a long series of de-icing trials with the Spitfire. Jeffrey sent me off to fly in any icing cloud I could find, but strange as it may seem although it was winter time I flew for hours without finding the conditions we were really looking for. In the end Jeffrey and I put our heads together in an effort to provide some device that would simulate the conditions we wanted.

I think the flying I most enjoyed in my early days at Southampton was the collection of a Walrus from Woolston for production trials. Taxying down the slipway into the water; slowly weaving between the large liners and warships with the company launch alongside in case of trouble; and then the wonderful feeling as the throttle was opened up and the waves and spray covered the hull and windscreen in a deluge of green sea-water. As we pulled off and the clatter of the hull and the swish of the water died away, below lay some of our magnificent ships—now the life blood of the nation.

Most pilots looked upon the Walrus as an ugly duckling and I may have thought the same. There was, however, something endearing about it. I am not sure if it was the incongruity amidst the sleek fighters and that I felt sorry for it, or that it operated in an environment which appealed to me and that when the going got rough it did its job like a professional. Certainly it was one of the noisiest, coldest and most uncomfortable machines I have ever flown and I never seemed to be able to climb in or out of the cramped cockpit without leaving a piece of skin behind. Strong it certainly was, and it could be landed on grass with the wheels up without much damage. I never tried this but George, on our first flight together, said, 'The Walrus is not for the absent-minded.' He then went on to tell me of pilots who had landed it in the water wheels down, or landed on the tarmac wheels up—both with spectacular results. I always felt you could land it on a postage stamp or in a puddle of water when you got used to its rather strange ungainly ways. At first it reminded me of a large iron dustbin filled with empty soup-tins: in rough water it seemed to float in about the same manner and with as much noise.

Operating in calm weather was pleasant, orthodox and easy. In really rough seas, however, I can only describe the experience as a wrestling match blindfolded. The noise of the waves pounding over the fore-deck, the hull hammering until it must surely cave in and the surging wind and water cascading over the cockpit was all rather frightening. As you peered through a constant stream of water over the screen and opened the throttle the first bout of wrestling was on. If a sudden huge wave hit you before you were ready, you throttled back, took another breath and waited your opportunity to plunge in again. The trick was to judge your wave roll accurately and to watch out for the heavy foaming tops that sometimes accompanied them. Although I was nearly always cold when I started this exercise, by the time I had kicked the rudder hard port and starboard a few dozen times, twisted, pushed and pulled the control column into my stomach, plunged through waves I felt sure would take us down to the ocean-bed and then finally hung on to the prop as I literally lifted this clattering tin-can into the air with the tail still clipping those furious waves below, I was in a bath of perspiration. But I loved every minute of it.

It was not often that George and I worked on the Walrus together. I think perhaps because of our age differences and also I think he was aware that Jeffrey and I were rather like mischievous schoolboys enjoying the fun of our work and that he gave us all the opportunities to do so. There were, unquestionably for me, moments when flying was at its best. Jeffrey and I once had some engine trials to do on the Walrus, necessitating a series of climbs from sea level to over 10,000 ft. The weather was clear below cloud but the overcast was thick. We decided for a variety of reasons, chiefly because of collision risk in cloud near other aerodromes, to go out to sea. We rattled down the Solent and then turned due south near Portsmouth, waited until past the Isle of Wight, and then started our first climb. There was a long period of concentration as first Jeffrey flew and I took down all the various temperatures, pressures, altitudes and speed, etc., and the Walrus was kept precisely at the right angle of attack with the dull grey cloud whirling over the wings as if in thick fog on the ground. We burst into brilliant sunshine completing the first run, paused, and then I took over the controls, diving into the gloom below in preparation for a repeat of the exercise. We did this several times, completely absorbed in our work. I do not think either of us had given a conscious thought to the fact that here we were, with a development engine, without any radio, a long way out at sea, and with the enemy almost within sight of us. I know I had complete trust and confidence in Jeffrey. This atmosphere, tinged probably subconsciously with tenseness and a certain amount of danger, created a bond, I felt, that is probably only equalled between brothers. At least this is how I felt, and it was a comradeship that I have rarely felt before or since.

Although I enjoyed the work, life was so different to what I had been accustomed that there were times when I felt the pang of homesickness. Barbara could only see me at weekends,

Dad came down about once every three weeks or so and of course I missed my labrador, Tony. I suppose this must have shown from time to time as Arthur Nelson was very considerate to me. He was the Eastleigh Works Manager: somewhat brusque in manner he went out of his way on many occasions to help me. George Pickering would nearly always go down to Woolston to the senior staff mess, with Jeffrey for lunch, where with the Managing Director, Commander Sir James Bird, Pratt, the General Manager, Joe Smith, the Chief Designer, and all the members of an old established team since the days of the famous designer R. J. Mitchell, they found much to talk about and discuss. I mostly had lunch on the aerodrome with Nelson, the head of AID and a few others; it was nothing like so good as the Woolston mess, but it took up less time. George was like an elder brother to me: nearly always he would come back and as I walked into the flight office after a series of tests he would often say, 'I told the canteen manager to pick me out the nicest apple for a very special friend', and he would hand me a beautiful apple, peach or pear or whatever happened to be in season at the time.

Barbara and I planned to get married in February, but we didn't want any fuss. The publicity had died down on outbreak of war and I was left in peace. Unfortunately I was prosecuted for exceeding the speed limit at about that time and the local papers got hold of it. In headlines they had printed 'Famous airman fined for speeding at 40 mph', and this of course started the phones ringing again and persistent enquiries as to when we were getting married, and where.

Supermarines had a contract to supply sixty Spitfires to Turkey and either Jeffrey or I would have to go there in the early part of the following year, so we spent a lot of time discussing how we were going to associate with the Germans, who were also, we understood, flying Messerschmitt 109s for the Turks at the same time. We reckoned we would have to go out by train, but that was before the war had hotted up and Italy had joined hands with Germany. Mutt Summers tried to get his own back on me for leaving Weybridge, by claiming they were overworked and wanted me back. Jeffrey and George were very good about this and were equally insistent that I was wanted with them. As I had promised Mutt I would help him out if he ever wanted me, however, I felt obliged to do something about it. Supermarines did not then have their own transport machine, so it meant that I had to travel by car or train if Bob Handasyde, one of the Weybridge technicians, rang me up and said they had a job for me to do. I was also pressed into testing the first Wellington from the new Chester factory, but occasionally Jeffrey allowed me to take one of the production or development Spitfires and kill two birds with one stone. If I went by train it was a long and tedious business which I did not enjoy.

In January I had a stupid little accident. After test and clearance by AID for delivery, Jeffrey and I would swing the compasses and make out the deviation cards for each machine; they were then towed from the flight shed to await collection from another hangar across the aerodrome. We were about to leave the flight shed when Len Levy the Superintendent asked if we could taxi the Spitfires over as the tractor had broken down. I had taken my flying gear off and I stepped into the machine and slid the hood over as it was wet and cold. I taxied onto the airfield and swung the machine in a series of turns that would enable me to see if anything was in the way. To my astonishment the next thing I knew was that my port wing was on top of a Fleet Air Arm Skua, the pilot of which had not seen me either and we came to an abrupt stop with my port wing looking the worst for wear. Annoyed with myself I made out the accident report and it was sent to Marsh-Hunn, the Commercial Manager of Supermarines. He did not like the way I had made out the report, however, and said, 'It puts all the blame on us.' I said, 'Well, it was my fault, and although you may juggle with words, I can only write what happened.'

We had now been able to find a house at Chandler's Ford,

by the unusual name of Tembani. Barbara had made arrangements for us to be married in Westminster Cathedral on the 17th of February. The press had got hold of this and were badgering Barbara and myself whenever they could find us. Barbara had a bright idea to hoodwink them and avoid all the ballyhoo of a publicised wedding. She arranged with a very helpful priest to publish the banns, which misled the press into thinking we could not get married before the official time of three weeks were up; we then obtained a special licence unknown to anyone. I drove up on the morning of the 17th in thick snow and ice and as Barbara and I walked into the precincts of Westminster Cathedral it was quiet and peaceful, the solemnity of the occasion undisturbed by the usual wailing of the air-raid sirens. As we made our vows the guns suddenly opened up and the sirens wailed and I realised I must hurry back to Southampton and carry on with the job. On the way back Barbara and I nearly finished up in hospital; the roads were covered with ice and snow and as I drove down Putney Hill a coal lorry backed out of a drive into the road in front of me. As I snatched the wheel over to avoid him the car spun round twice with the bonnet sweeping under the tail of the lorry and we came to an abrupt standstill in a pile of snow, shaken but otherwise unhurt.

The winter of 1939/40 was hard and cold. Jeffrey had mapped out an area in which we were to test and all the local defences were made aware of our activities. As a rule after donning Mae Wests the drill was to follow the Hamble river to the Solent, proceed along the shore at Lee-on-Solent, turn due south near Portsmouth and enter the Channel leaving the Isle of Wight on the starboard side. In February of 1940 we had not yet suffered our defeat leading to Dunkirk and a surge of tremendous pride would always sweep through me as I swooped low over those magnificent ships of the line; as I thought of them upholding our Naval fighting traditions dating back to Drake and beyond, I was conscious that I did so in the finest fighting aircraft in the world at the time.

The name Rolls-Royce was synonymous with quality and reliability. At the time a forced landing through engine failure with a Merlin was almost unheard of. Jeffrey had had an engine failure in a Spitfire pre-war and as I think he would now agree, one would have thought it was the greatest calamity since the Civil War. Little did I know what was in store for me. As it happened there were few incidents of real note that I recollect. The worst for me was during a test dive when I struck a seagull, which sounded like a bullet striking the wing. It did not affect the feel of the aircraft and I returned to Eastleigh. When I stepped from the machine to see what the others were gaping at I was shocked; the bird had struck the wing on the leading edge at the strongest section, near the fuselage, and it had made a hole like a cannon shell. The gory mess of blood, flesh and feathers was embedded inside some ten or twelve inches. Jeffrey and I looked at each other and said, 'We shall have to be more careful'; but this was not easy as there were large flocks of seagulls around most of the time.

Jeffrey was an exceptional pilot, particularly at aerobatics. I rated him amongst the best in the world. He was contemptuous of imperfections and did not discourage me from doing things that today would be considered suicidal, and warrant the suspension of one's licence forthwith. It was more than common for one of us to approach Eastleigh at high speed, usually after a satisfactory test flight, roll over into the inverted below the height of the flight shed, push the nose up to miss the roof, put the undercarriage down as we did so, roll over to the normal position, lower the flaps and land all in one smooth clean sweep.

The Fleet Air Arm who controlled the aerodrome at Eastleigh were extremely tolerant and lived in the spirit of the moment and I never at any time received a complaint or in fact ever heard of one. Our flight office was small and a little dingy. We had three desks and a telephone, and to liven things up I had brought a wireless set from home, which George and Jeffrey agreed improved things somewhat. In an adjoining office were representatives of the Ministry of Aircraft Production (MAP) and each day they sent a report to the London office. Unfortunately, for a period they were unable to obtain their own phone, so permission was given for them to use ours. This soon became annoying in the extreme. We would be working on written reports in deep silence, or, if not pressed, be having a quiet discussion with some soft background music, when in would stamp the Ministry representative; for the next quarter of an hour we would hear him bellowing to London as if he had made and flown the aircraft himself. Jeffrey was the first to put his thoughts into words: 'We must do something about it.' I certainly needed no prompting. I do not remember quite how we did it, but we rigged our wireless set to the phone and had a special switch which we could operate when the Ministry man came in. The first time he used our trap we allowed him to get through to London and then pulled the switch; the look on his face was indescribable. I buried my head in my arms on the desk, and saw Jeffrey stuffing a handkerchief into his mouth to suppress his laughter. We heard a voice spluttering back through the phone: 'What the hell's going on down there? All I can hear is Vera Lynn.' Of course it was reported to the GPO, but they couldn't find anything wrong as our wires were outside the office and the switch did not show. We let him have another undisturbed call or so and then we wired the set in a different manner: he got through to London again and this time as we pulled the switch the office was filled with Stanford Robinson playing 'In a 15th-century drawing room'—with the sound coming out of the mouthpiece of the phone. Jeffrey and I had to go outside as we were bursting our sides. The poor man came rushing out soon afterwards, swearing and cursing the GPO and I suspect us, for that was the last time he ever used our phone.

One day when the weather was bad Jeffrey and I decided to drive to Heston to see the set-up established by Sidney Cotton, which I had so nearly joined. Cotton was certainly right about his powers; he had commandeered several important aircraft, including Spitfires, and on the day we arrived had in fact been given one of the first constant-speed airscrew control units, something we had not yet got on our own Spitfires. We were quite impressed with his organisation, but not very long after someone else took over and the organisation went on to become the Photographic Reconnaissance Unit famous throughout the war.

I was fully absorbed in the work and found the experimental side and the discussions with members of the design and technical staff at Woolston interesting and stimulating.

When we were not flying I helped Jeffrey repair and paint his clinker-built dinghy, which he kept in another part of the hangar at Eastleigh. He lived near the aerodrome and occasionally Barbara would spend the day with Pat, Jeffrey's wife, with us joining them later on. We were now comfortably settled at Chandler's Ford and as spring approached we began to think of a normal life. Jeffrey said to me one day, 'You know Alex, I think this phoney war is going to fizzle out.' I must say in many ways it rather looked like that. To keep fit I got Dad to send Beauty down to us. A grey mare, she had won both the hunter and jumping classes at the Dublin Horse Show and was suitable for both Barbara and myself. Early in the morning or in the evening I would take Tony and would go for a canter in the lovely wooded country at the foot of the downs. When the weather warmed Jeffrey and I went sailing in the Solent and about that time Pat and he decided to buy a charming little house on the slopes overlooking the Hamble river.

The Walrus development programme was idyllic work in such surroundings. After always having to pay for my flying, sometimes very expensively, I sometimes marvelled that I should now be sent a cheque each month for doing so. In the warm spring sunshine, landing trials in the clear blue waters with the spray leaving a telltale wake as we climbed steeply into the radiant sky was flying at its best, and I wondered if this was really my true vocation. Such was our light-heartedness that Jeffrey said one day: 'We ought to do some fishing, with this set of long Walrus trials on.' I took him at his word, acquired some hooks and lines and asked Arthur Nelson to get us some lugworms. I think Jeffrey thought I had taken him too literally, but in any case we never caught any fish.

4 ✳ *Chief Pilot, Castle Bromwich*

ONE DAY the whole country was shaken from its comfortable lethargy as the German blitz crashed through France. We now knew our thoughts had been wishful: there was an urgency which previously had been missing and a grim picture began to emerge. As Europe fell under the German hordes we began to feel very much alone and knew in a matter of days we would be fighting with our backs to the wall. We saw a grimmer picture than most in England at that time as we flew day after day down the Solent into the Channel. We saw the remains of what had once been a proud fighting unit, now scattered with only the uniforms they stood up in, bloodied and torn as they slumped on the decks of British ships of all types. These limped into Southampton Water, some with their superstructure damaged, some with shellholes down to the waterline and one, a destroyer with its propeller shot away, being towed in by another damaged ship. In they all crawled at what seemed to me from the air to be a snail's pace. Troops were everywhere and the wounded were quickly and quietly loaded onto trains, which took them to hospitals all over the country. The Local Defence Volunteers had been formed, later to become known as the Home Guard, and a great many were getting jittery and kept their fingers too close to the trigger for comfort.

We had recently taken over the test flying of Spitfires after repair at the Morris Motors Cowley works near Oxford and also the first machines from the enormous shadow factory at Castle Bromwich were beginning to emerge. I used to drive to both these places by car, as all our aircraft had to be put into active service as soon as possible. I always took Barbara with me as the feeling was there that anything could happen at any moment. The road blocks were tiresome and rather pathetic, sometimes just a light pole attached to a cartwheel guarded by two civilians with armbands of the LDV and carrying a shotgun or maybe only a pitchfork. My priority identification pass permitted me to go almost anywhere so we were not much delayed.

As the pressure built up so we worked harder and longer hours. Panic was almost taking over at Castle Bromwich. They rang one evening for me to go there immediately to fly their second production Spitfire. I asked if the machine was actually waiting to be flown and was told no, but it would be ready by the time I arrived. I promised to be there at first light in the morning. Barbara and I snatched a few hours sleep and set off at about 1 o'clock next morning. We saw the first streaks of light creeping into the sky as we topped the rise near Edgehill and I accelerated as fast as I dared in the dim morning light, saying to Barbara, 'They'll wonder where the hell I've got to.' As we drove into the Castle Bromwich works two of the main factory doors were open and sure enough there was the Spitfire outside on the tarmac, almost hidden from view as dozens of workmen and inspectors literally crawled in, over and around it. Talamo, the General Manager, and E. R. Scales, the Assembly Block Superintendent greeted us and apologised for the aircraft not being ready for flight, but if we would go into Birmingham and have some breakfast, it would be ready when we returned. Barbara and I had a wash, a good meal and then returned to the factory. The picture had not changed a great deal, except the crowd of workmen had been joined by Alex Dunbar, Air Commodore Verney, Mr Wickham the chief of AID and the Works Manager, Bernard Cook. If the position had not been so critical and so serious it would have been laughable: Dunbar and the others would hang around the machine; everyone was getting in everyone else's way with Dunbar or Talamo picking up a screwdriver and making attempts to drive home the Oddy cowling fasteners on one side, whilst the inspectors or workmen on the other hand were taking them out. Eventually they both realised what was going on. There was nothing I could do; I had left a hefty programme at Eastleigh, but Dunbar would not let me leave until I had flown the Spitfire. We hung around all day.

At last as the June sun sank slowly in the sky the solitary Spitfire Mark II was towed out onto the airfield. Anxious and tired people followed it looking both at me and the machine with an air of expectancy. At least half a dozen men were still putting the finishing touches under the supervision of works and AID inspectors as I stepped into the cockpit. To my surprise the aircraft flew extremely well and responded like the thoroughbred it was. After several minor adjustments I felt able to finish off with the usual aerobatic display. As the heat went out of the day mist banks formed on the surface of the airfield. In a low run in front of the small crowd I cut a clean swathe through the mist and as I climbed away I saw that in the still air the clear path was slow to fill in.

I had flown consistently since my move to Eastleigh eight months previously so I had by this time got to know the Spitfire well. With the eruption of war and the recent shock of the collapse of France and our other Allies in Europe, all crushed so violently by the mailed fist of the Nazi, I had become, like so many other young men, imbued with the spirit of the time in which we were living and I tackled everything with a vigorous determination which many might have called aggression. The thought came that these people below had worked day and night to produce this solitary machine, whilst Germany had thousands ready to invade us. My own contribution seemed so insignificant that the best I could do was to show them, not just a mild aerobatic performance, but the real precision and outstanding capabilities of our finest fighting machine. I set my finishing flight-path to run parallel to the clear line that still showed plainly between the mist banks and dived at a speed which would give me very positive rudder control as I rolled over the vertical, but not so high that the ailerons became too heavy. I levelled out almost on the thin

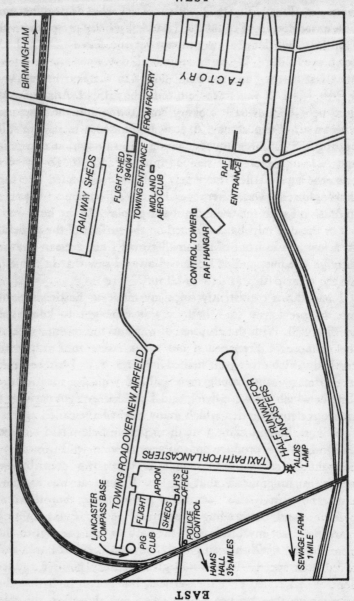

Castle Bromwich airfield

white blanket that partially covered the ground. I was told later it was about head height; in fact those sitting on car roofs said they could see over the top of the fogbanks.

Many pilots criticise the execution of aerobatics at low altitudes. In fact on my first flight my instructor seriously lectured me and said, 'Only fools aerobat close to the ground: it is highly dangerous; it proves nothing and is pure exhibitionism.' Certainly I have seen several skilled pilots roll themselves into the ground and in some instances one is not too sure as to what exactly went wrong. Possibly if the pilots had lived one could have learned the fatal error but as one is working within such narrow and delicate margins perhaps the pilots themselves were unaware of their mistake.

Ordinarily, the Spitfire rolls with astonishing ease, but as every skilled pilot knows, the variation and range of a roll is infinite. One can roll with the simplicity of a turn; one can induce a little negative 'G' or in fact, if required, no negative 'G' at all; one can smoothly and gracefully execute roll after roll after roll with the delight of a dolphin in the blue and white surge of the Pacific Ocean and from the ground it will look accurate and precise. There is however a vast difference between this light-hearted frolic and that of a high-speed roll a few feet from the ground, when the procedure is entirely different—the use of co-ordination, precision and judgement calling for the highest degree of concentration.

It is strange how few pilots realise how much room is required to execute a roll no matter how 'tight' around the horizontal axis. I found this out in my early days when being filmed from another aircraft. I was to fly in formation and then at a given signal from the photographer, I was to perform a neat roll to starboard which would come out in glorious technicolour. To my surprise the radius of my roll, fortunately away from the other machine, was such that I went out of view of the camera. Since then I have, I think, learned a great deal.

In a normal roll with a Spitfire, with height to spare, the use of the rudder, if need be, can almost be ignored. Not so at low altitude. On that beautiful summer evening in 1940, as I crossed the airfield eastern boundary, the nose of the Spitfire was sighted, like a rifle, at the Midlands Aero Club black roof over on the other side. As the ailerons were slowly but very firmly moved to starboard, the control column in conjunction was eased forward and then as the aircraft approached the critical moment of inversion the rudder would be coming in to act as elevator to keep that nose exactly on target. As the machine slowly turned into the fully inverted position, with the alteration in the angle of attack, the nose was now sighted slightly above the clubhouse roof and the rudder resumed its proper purpose and kept the aircraft precisely on line. I always felt that the Spitfire should be held for a short spell in this position with all controls, as one might say, neutralised, to give the opportunity to prepare for the exacting process the other way while from the corner of my eyes I adjusted to the altered orientation. In this instance I kept the nose slightly above the ground mist but the fin seemed to be cutting a swathe right through it. Just before the target of the clubhouse was reached the machine was slowly but accurately rolled to complete the 360° and finish with a turn for landing over the buildings on the west side of the aerodrome.

One accepts that the concentration for this type of extremely low demonstration is of a very high order and one could not afford to make a single mistake. If I had any worries at that time, it was that the harness might move slightly, as it sometimes did if a buckle was fouled on the armour-plate or seat, so that I always stretched and tested it well beforehand. Another disconcerting feature could be the fall of swarf from the bottom of the fuselage when not cleaned properly in the factory and the danger of a metal fragment getting into my eyes, as I would never roll close to the ground with my goggles on.

As I touched down in one of the clear patches and taxied up to the little crowd I could see that it had had the desired effect. All were now talking animatedly to one another. The Station

Commander had at first been somewhat bewildered at this crowd of civilians invading his aerodrome over whom he had neither control nor jurisdiction, and as a result had adopted a rather quiet, aloof and dignified manner; now he was talking excitedly to Alex Dunbar and Mr Talamo whilst wiping the sweatband of his hat with his handkerchief.

I was anxious to get away and make as good time as I could before the light went altogether; we were driving very fast on the outskirts of Kenilworth when a man in civilian clothes waved me down. Thinking he wanted a lift I murmured to Barbara, 'He'll be unlucky, we're in too much of a hurry to pick up passengers.' Almost at the same time Barbara let out a yell for me to stop. I slammed on the brakes to see a policeman come from behind a tree, raise a revolver and take aim. As we squealed to a standstill he was still pointing the revolver at me, demanding to know why I had not stopped when told to do so by a Home Guard officer. Just then the civilian ran up and I saw the armband. I couldn't find enough words in my vocabulary to tell them what I thought about the Kenilworth police, Home Guard and everything else that came to mind, but it was typical of those early days that an armband was the only means of recognition.

The first machines to be produced at Castle Bromwich were Mark IIs. There were many improvements on the old Mark I, the most important of which was the elimination of the large pump-handle and the fitting of a power-operated control for the undercarriage. A constant-speed airscrew had been fitted— the old two-position plunger type control was inadequate under certain conditions, particularly in combat flying; and it could also be misused to the detriment of the engine. We often used to juggle the valve control in flight to get maximum power without exceeding engine limitations but I never felt very happy about it.

I had hoped that the aileron control on the new Mark IIs would be better. On my earliest flights in the Spitfire I felt the controls were light and well harmonised. I had no reason to change my mind until I started to use combat manoeuvres at high speeds or perform aerobatics and then I found the ailerons excessively heavy. At that time they were fabric covered, as were all the control surfaces, and had to be flight rigged with short lengths of cord doped underneath or on top of the trailing edges. They had the bad habit of distorting or slacking off when parked out in bad weather conditions and as a result the machine would fly one wing low until rectified. Another weakness I did not like was that on old machines the control wires were often slack. In a dive, if excessive aileron force was used, one could see the fabric ballooning but there were also times when the ailerons became overbalanced and would have to be changed. When first I heard vague whispers of structural failures in the Spitfire I wondered at times if this could have been a contributory cause. When we later received the metal-covered ailerons, the situation was much improved as we could then dress the trailing edges up or down and did not have to rely upon dope and cord for rigging.

I think all of us at Supermarines were conscious of these early shortcomings and I know we used the Mark III prototype with its clipped wings to improve the roll rate and performance; but as I remember, the spoilt looks did not provide the improvement expected. By this time the Merlin XII was being used and gave the Spitfire Mark II a slightly better take-off and climb.

Jeffrey, George and I decided we must work shifts around the clock and we each took it in turn on a rota basis. I rather liked the early morning stint, as this meant a take-off at first light and I could see the sun rise over the sea. One morning as the first red streaks appeared in the east I was suddenly jolted out of my still somewhat dreamy state by the silhouette of two seaplanes well apart but flying from the Channel and moving in the direction of Woolston. I knew we had no seaplanes in operation and all I could think of was the German Blohm and Voss used for mine-laying and torpedo work. My first reaction was that they had to be stopped at all costs: I had no radio to call the defences; we were not then fitted with guns; but as they were making for the docks, shipping and possibly our own factory, it was up to me to do something. I decided to ram one. Then I thought if I went down with the first machine the other would still get through. We were fitted with VP metal air-screws so I reasoned there might be a chance of me putting the elevators out of action on one machine and then leaving me undamaged to deal with the other. I approached the nearest machine with the sun at my back but couldn't see any torpedo, bombs or gun turret. I guessed there would be one in the fuselage somewhere so I dropped a little lower and then opened the throttle to approach as fast as I dared in time to slow up so that my airscrew would bite into the tail without putting me completely out of action. As I manoeuvred into position I was puzzled by the lack of opposition: no guns had been fired, no evasive action taken. Perhaps, I thought, in the early morning light and the brittle sunshine they had not seen me. Approaching closer and closer I looked for the swastika before I rammed. At that moment the seaplane made a slight turn and there on the fuselage and wings I saw the Dutch insignia. Relieved beyond measure, I swung in close formation and the pilots and occupants gave me a vigorous wave. When I returned to Eastleigh to report the matter I learned that the Dutch Royal Family and some of the government had been rescued by the Royal Navy and others had escaped to England by air. Catastrophic events were happening.

I was now involved in the production and experimental flying at Southampton, chasing off by car to Castle Bromwich, Chester or Cowley when required. The Cowley works were, as far as I could see, very efficiently run by a Mr Cullum. The Tiger Moths built and repaired there were flown by a pilot from de Havillands; the repaired Hurricanes by a Hawker pilot. In that early summer of 1940 the Hawker pilot was Dick Reynell;* he was a grand fellow and we were soon firm friends. His blue eyes would look straight into your face and he had the

* Later to be killed in the Battle of Britain.

ability and courage that would make anyone proud to have known him.

When Lord Beaverbrook became Minister of Aircraft Production he immediately commandeered most of the aircraft being used for research and development and at Supermarines we had a number of these allocated for various test-flying programmes. Now this policy was very severely criticised at the time and has been since. Some take the view that the policy was shortsighted, inasmuch as it held up important design and developments on later machines as well as the production of prototypes. I have always held the view that Beaverbrook was right: if we were so short of fighting machines at such a critical stage in our defence and we lost the battle because we did not throw in everything we had, we might easily have lost the entire war. Nothing would have been of any further use then.

Early in the year I was offered the post of Chief Pilot at Castle Bromwich, but turned it down. I did not like the idea of working for a vast sausage-machine turning out aircraft; I enjoyed the mixed type of flying at Southampton and worked very well with Jeffrey and George. When Barbara and I had done about a dozen trips to Birmingham, however, we both remarked how well we felt and how much more energy we had during our brief stops in the Midlands. We both found that at Southampton we had to force ourselves to play any sport, to do any gardening was an effort, and any spare time was spent lying around semi-exhausted. The outcome was that we looked around the Midlands with a different eye and when Barbara said she would prefer to live there, I went back and asked if I could withdraw my refusal. This was accepted and shortly after there was a group pilots' meeting at Weybridge, attended by Alex Dunbar and Major Hew Kilner. One of the chief problems to be discussed was the effect of winter weather on a heavy wartime flying programme; McNichol who had only just joined the firm said that when he worked at the Austin Fairey Battle works at Longbridge near Birmingham, there had been periods as long as six weeks when they had not left the ground. Mutt Summers turned to me and with a grin said, 'You're going to enjoy yourself.' In July we moved to a rented house in Streetly, on the outskirts of Birmingham.

Certainly that summer was heaven-sent, we borrowed the Flight Shed at times from the Royal Air Force at Castle Bromwich, but in reality our workshop was a large box on an open field and my office the inside of the car. In the June of that year Castle Bromwich had produced ten Spitfires after tremendous pressure from Beaverbrook on Dunbar and others, that had almost reduced them to nervous wrecks. This momentous occasion was called 'The ten in June' and was so inscribed on a number of cigarette lighters to those privileged to deserve one.

Castle Bromwich was as much like Supermarines as chalk is to cheese; although Barbara and I felt better in health, I found the work in such an atmosphere terribly trying. In addition to Castle Bromwich I was given Morris Motors at Cowley, whose Spitfire repair output was building up and also a new repair unit for Wellingtons based at Sywell; this was now managed by my old friend Tommy Bancroft, who had once done a job on my Comper Swift engine during the London–Newcastle race. I soon realised that to get through my programme I must have a transport aircraft and Alex Dunbar gave me the go-ahead to get one.

Every day we expected the invasion as the bombing got worse day and night. We fared better in the day than Supermarines, but at night I felt sure it could not go on for much longer without something cracking. The Germans seemed to find the factory at Castle Bromwich almost every time and one got hardened to the sight of a direct hit on, say, the machine shop before all employees had gone into the shelters; as day slowly dawned it was common to find bits of bodies mingled with valuable equipment blasted to small pieces and hanging gruesomely from what had been the roof. The spirit of the British people at that time was magnificent and quite irrepressible and within days there would be a temporary roof on, new machines would be moved in and the shop would be back into production. One of the worst weapons of that summer was the delayed action bomb. These were scattered all over the place, particularly on the aerodrome and around the factory, and it was a little disconcerting when taking off for one to suddenly explode nearby.

I had only a few mechanics to work on the flight side at that time, but what I had were good. I knew I should need many more soon and started to look around for suitable men. The engine side was taken care of by Rolls-Royce themselves; at first I thought their Chief Mechanic, Dodds, would come up from Southampton. I did not always hit it off too well with Dodds: his diagnosis for engine trouble was invariably 'Effing plugs.' Just before I had left Supermarines I had had my first forced landing in a Spitfire. I was carrying out full-throttle level runs at 24,000 ft and could see Bristol and the south coast clearly below. I was having to hang on to the level runs a little longer with the throttle and revs wide open to obtain accurate readings, as the conditions were not ideal, when I thought I detected a slight change in the note of the engine. I was taking constant readings of oil pressure, oil and glycol temperatures, so I knew without re-checking that these were OK yet I had the feeling that the engine was going to blow up in my face and I snapped the throttle back without more ado. My first reaction was to land at Boscombe Down, which I could reach easily, and then I thought I might stretch my glide to reach Eastleigh as the wind was in my favour. I made it with not much to spare and as I came to a standstill on the aerodrome I was more than pleased with myself. Dodds, Levy and Jeffrey came out to me and I explained what had happened. Dodds said immediately, 'Effing plugs; I'll start the engine and see which one it is.' I snapped angrily, 'If you think I've done a dead-stick landing from 24,000 ft for you to undo all I have tried to save, you'd better think again.' Jeffrey, I think, was the only one who took me seriously and he said, 'Drop the oil filters before you restart the engine.' They did so and there were enough white metal bits inside to need no further explanation as to what had happened. In the event Rolls sent Dodds' number one to Castle Bromwich.

5 ✳ *Showing off the Spitfire*

AT SOUTHAMPTON distinguished visitors were some-what rare. In most cases they went to the Woolston office unless it was a special mission, such as the French Air Force Group headed by Detroyet; then George put on a show with the Walrus and Jeffrey flew the Mark III, whilst I flew the Mark I Spitfire.

I am not sure how impressive the show looked from the ground. The plan had been for George to fly the Walrus past the French mission at the slowest possible speed with wheels retracted and the hull very close to the ground. I was to watch from about 2000 ft and dive past the Walrus when it was opposite the group; Jeffrey, who was stationed above me, would do the same thing. The Walrus would then land and Jeffrey and I would carry out a series of individual aerobatics. I have a feeling we could have done better. I never realised until that moment how slow a Walrus could fly in competent hands, nor did I appreciate the speed of the Spitfire in a dive, so that I misjudged badly and flashed past George about 20 yards before he had reached the distinguished party, their gold braid glinting in the winter sunshine. My premature move of course misled Jeffrey and he did the same thing. Certainly those below were extremely impressed by Jeffrey and the Mark III: it was faster and had a better roll rate than my Mark I and we had purposely planned the flying sequences to show a much better rate of climb with our latest machine.

At Castle Bromwich I was called on constantly to show off the qualities of the Spitfire and was to do so on innumerable occasions for the next six years. It was rare that I objected to this; in fact I often relished taking the breath away from Americans, Russians, Swedes, French, Norwegians and many other groups who came expecting not to be impressed. I soon realised that I was used by the management in a rather nice nonchalant manner on these occasions and many, particularly journalists in aviation, came to obtain a free interview with me.

On 18 September 1940 Alex Dunbar rang me at my office and said, 'Alex, we are trying to support the Lord Mayor of Birmingham with a Spitfire fund and I promised him you would put on a show.' I said, 'Of course, sir. I'll have a machine ready on the airfield right away. When is he due to arrive?' Dunbar replied, 'He's not coming to us. He's making an appeal on the steps of the Civic Centre and I would like you to perform over the ceremony as I think this will draw attention to the appeal in a most appropriate manner.' When I had caught my breath I said, 'Don't you think we are taking a bit of a chance? If I have an engine failure, it is going to be a bit awkward. And I don't think the police are going to think much of it.' He went on, 'Oh, I've fixed all that with the Lord Mayor. You've nothing to worry about.' And put the receiver down. I was thoroughly angry on several counts: I had joined the firm to test aircraft and not to put on exhibitions; I was taking a big risk as Birmingham is as large a built-up area as one was likely to find in the country; I had not been consulted about this palsy-walsy arrangement between Dunbar and the Lord Mayor, who probably didn't know a Spitfire from a Tiger Moth. In fact, I felt I was being used.

I started off at 5000 ft spot on the prearranged time. I didn't like it at all, as all I could see below were miles and miles of factories and houses: where I could put down if I had to, I didn't know. At first I was just angry with what I thought was a stupid, unsafe arrangement; then as I pointed my nose vertically to plunge in a dive over the city, the Civic Centre, being new and white, stood out clearly in the smoke begrimed background. I thought, I'll teach Dunbar and the Lord Mayor something they'll not forget in a hurry. Having used up all my surplus height in a series of vertical upward rolls, I shot down the main street of Birmingham rolling as I did and finished in the inverted position below the top of the Civic Centre. I heard afterwards that the effect on the city was petrifying: all the buses and cars came to a standstill, people opened offices, ran from the doors, peered out of the windows; and crowds came onto the roads to get a better view. The police could not control the chaos. That evening in the local paper was a very good photograph of the Spitfire with the Civic Centre in the background, and the headline 'rolling to victory'.

When I returned to Castle Bromwich, I had just climbed down from the cockpit when the first batch of police cars started to arrive; the first to reach me was the Chief Constable, with almost a dozen deputies. He demanded to know who the pilot was shooting up the city centre; I replied, calmer than I felt, 'I was.' He said, 'I'm afraid you will have to come with me and make a statement.' I said, 'I'm not going anywhere and I'm certainly not making a statement. I suggest you get in touch with your Lord Mayor and ask him what the position is. As far as I'm concerned I take my instructions from my Managing Director.' Just when the matter was about to become argumentative, Lord Dudley arrived, whom I knew very well. He said to the police, 'Just leave us for a few moments, will you,' and took me to one side. 'Christ, Henshaw,' he said, 'you've put the cat amongst the pigeons this time. Do you know you brought the whole of Birmingham to a standstill, and some of my people are writing to the Prime Minister thinking it was an air-raid.' I apologised and told him what had happened. He then left with the police and that was the last I heard of the affair, but I was never again asked to put on a show unless I was first consulted about the arrangements.

Barbara and I were not very happy in a rented house, so we started to look around for one to buy. We wanted to be in the country and eventually found a delightful little house in Hampton-in-Arden. It was owned by a local estate agent, and he had built on four stables, a coachhouse and loft with a beautiful landscaped garden and grass paddock adjoining. The whole property was architect designed and we loved it.

Our losses in aircraft during training periods were extremely high, particularly with the Spitfire. Alex Dunbar said to me one day that he had been talking to the Chief of Fighter Command and thought that if I went round to some of the Operational Training Units and demonstrated the Spitfire it would do a great deal of good. I didn't enthuse over the idea but said if I received a request from an OTU I would of course be pleased to go. The first visit was to Hawarden, which had changed into one of the most important OTUs in the country for final Spitfire training. Here as well as hundreds of novice trainees were some of the best pilots in the Air Force; I was fully aware that whilst I might have got away creditably with some wild aerial gyrations in front of an ill-informed group, this time my audience would be critical. In fact some might welcome the opportunity to pick holes in a young amateur.

These demonstrations over the years varied according to the audience and the conditions. Like providing a good seat at the cinema the first thing to do if possible was to fly with the sun on the backs of the audience, so that they were not blinded all the time, and at a distance which did not make them strain their necks. Always if I could I operated up and down wind: if the wind was strong and one upward-rolled across it, the manoeuvre could look untidy, and sometimes would put one in the incorrect position for the next manoeuvre. As a rule the drill was to take off and not climb but pause with the wheels coming up and the machine just clear of the ground and at 150–160 IAS pull up slowly but firmly into a half loop finishing with a half roll at the top. I never really liked this as one cough from the engine and I should have been in real trouble; at the roll stage I was in any case holding the machine by maximum engine power well below the normal stall and the slightest coarse handling on the controls would cause the machine to flick out.

I would continue this in maybe another couple of half loops and rolls until I was over 4000 ft and then placing myself in the correct position over the aerodrome, half roll again and go into an absolutely vertical dive with full engine and maximum revs to pull out a few feet from the ground and go into a vertical roll to the left, a vertical roll to the right and a half roll to the left with a half loop, and then pull out to repeat the manoeuvre in the opposite direction. Pulling out in another half loop in the other direction, the throttle would be snapped back and plummeting down vertically one could get in two complete aileron turns to pull out again and open the throttle to do the same thing in the other direction. Having now used up most of my height and speed, I would pull up vertically to about 1000 ft and in a tight half loop at the right moment flick the machine into a full flick roll. This I always felt was a tricky one. It took a lot of judging to do it accurately, because very often the manoeuvre was so sudden and vicious that on checking the machine it would be sometimes slightly out of line and I knew it could look untidy. I could usually get one-and-a-half to two full flicks of a roll on the horizontal but for the sake of control and tidiness I usually settled for one, which I knew I could judge to a nicety. In practice I could get in about the same with the vertical flick rolls, but I found these almost impossible for me to judge, when to check and to come out clean. I have never seen anyone flick-roll a Spitfire and I must say that I always found it a little frightening to abuse a machine and have it flash out of your control, if only for a few seconds, like a young spirited blood-horse.

On the pull-out from the flick-roll, sometimes I would open the engine flat out in another vertical climb and at approximately 1200 ft push the nose over forward and with the engine closed complete the half of an outside loop, usually in those days called a 'bunt'. I never really liked this manoeuvre either; it was easy but required heavy pressure forward on the control column and you could not afford to misjudge at 1200 ft: with the nose going over down towards the ground the speed built up at such an alarming rate that it left no room to change your mind until it was too late. At the bottom of the inverted dive I would usually 'round off' to a few feet above the ground and then with as much pressure as I dare use on the control column—I say 'dare' because I found it more disconcerting and frightening to 'black-out' from excessive negative 'G' than I did from high loads in the positive position—I would push the machine into an almost vertical climb and then as it lost momentum from the negative 'G' position, pull the control gently over to form a half-loop, hoping as I did that the engine would burst into life as I opened the throttle. This it usually did with a spectacular sheet of flame pluming from the exhaust stubs caused by unused fuel which had accumulated during the inverted manoeuvres. With the engine now on full power I would do a series of very low rolls left and right in front of the audience at below hangar height finishing in the inverted position from which I would 'raise' the undercarriage, pull into a tight, fast engine-off turn and lower the flaps as I touched down for the landing.

I was welcomed at Hawarden, courteously. After a short chat about the object of the exercise, I took off somewhat expectantly as the Commanding Officer said he had not bothered to stop all the flying: he expected I would only be a few minutes. I flew my best without taking undue risks and not cutting my margins too fine. I think I felt at the time that my show might have been all right but could have been better as part of my concentration was broken looking out for stray aircraft. When I landed any apprehension I may have felt was quickly dispelled as I glanced at the faces of the senior officers surrounded by numerous young enthusiastic OTU pilots all surging forward to greet me. Wing Commander Donaldson was the first to speak: 'I've seen them all, but if I had not been here today I would never have believed a Spitfire could fly like that,' he said. Naturally I was relieved and very satisfied, but as it was then coming on to rain I made my excuses and had a wet, uncomfortable flight back to Castle Bromwich, where Barbara waited for me patiently with our lunch ruined.

We were all more and more jittery as each day passed through this glorious summer. We bought the house in Hampton-in-Arden and renamed it 'The Ridings'. Barbara and I dashed up one day to London for a few hours and in between the air-raids and stepping over heaps of debris we bought enough furniture and carpets in that short while to complete the house so that we could at least move in.

As I was about to take off in a Spitfire the following morning, Squadron Leader Modley, the Castle Bromwich aerodrome commander, rushed over to me by car and shouted, 'Alex, there's a Fairey Battle taking photographs over Birmingham; it's unidentified and they think it's a Jerry!' I grabbed a Very pistol and two cartridges and rushed off. At first I could not see the machine and then in the distance I saw the Fairey Battle at about 10,000 ft well to the west of the city. I closed in and pointed to the pilot to go down. He took no notice, so I pushed back the cockpit hood and fired the Very pistol in front of him and then slid behind his tail so that he would think I was going to blast him out of the sky. He came down quickly enough when he saw what I was doing so that we landed together. I pointed out the control tower to the Battle pilot and in wide formation we taxied over to Squadron Leader Modley, who had the support of several other RAF officers and a squad of men with rifles at the ready. I jumped out expecting some excitement, only to hear Modley apologising to the pilot of the Battle and saying that someone had made a mistake. Naturally enough the pilot having got over his first fright did not look at all pleased to see me.

Anxious that there should be no delay in testing and as the Spitfire was then fitted with landing lights, I continued flying at odd times, if necessary into the night. I had to take great care as with the blackout it was very easy to miss the aerodrome and get lost. To me in retrospect, the atmosphere at the time was a little unreal. We all felt invasion was imminent; those that had any degree of knowledge knew that we could not stop it, and those who had the courage accepted the cold fact that we were going to be defeated. That did not mean throwing up the sponge, but each one of us had personal problems and thoughts that were never disclosed, even to those closest. I was determined for my part that there would be no surrender, but how I would really face up to this I had to leave to some extent until the time came. In the meantime I felt it was up to every individual to give of his best at whatever he was doing, and I flew day in and day out for months, almost without a break. In the late summer sky I looked below at all the cricket matches going on during the Saturdays and Sundays, and even sometimes during midweek, and I could not help thinking that many were unaware of the true situation.

On 6 September I returned from Scotland, having acquired a 3-seater Percival Gull for communications, to be greeted by Barbara and Dad and Squadron Leader Modley. I could tell from the looks on their faces that something very serious had happened. 'They're here! I've just had the purple signal,' shouted Modley. Fortunately I had cleared all the Spitfires before I had left for Scotland and the only thing for me to do was to prepare the demolition of everything that might be useful to the enemy, and then grab what weapons we could get hold of and wait. We had no Home Guard at that time worthwhile and very few weapons, so our situation against well-equipped paratroops was really pathetic. We waited tense and anxious, little being said. Then the phone suddenly rang and we were told the purple was withdrawn but the red was still on; a little later the phone rang again giving all clear. It was some time before I heard the reason for all these false alarms.

The bombing had compelled production dispersal and I now had units to cover at Desford and Cosford as well as Cowley and Sywell. It had been arranged for another of the firm's pilots, George Snarey, as soon as the work justified, to join me. George was a very nice fellow. He had just left Westlands, where they were producing the Lysander. Prior to this he was a Flight Lieutenant in the RAF and I should imagine a very good officer. Also joining Vickers-Armstrongs at Castle Bromwich at that time as overseer was a Wing Commander Thompson. I was great friends with Tommy. He was one of the few overseers in my experience who seemed to know what an overseer's duties should be, and was helpful and co-operative without being obtrusive. After my experience in September, when we waited like sitting ducks to be killed by the Germans, I suggested to him that there should now be enough spare Spitfires for us to gun up as protection for ourselves; he agreed and we went over to Wittering in the Gull to discuss the matter with Group Captain Embry.* He had recently escaped from France and had strangled a German with his bare hands to do so. I liked him and our discussion was very amicable but not very useful: he insisted that any fighters based at Castle Bromwich for factory defence must come under Fighter Command and the pilots also. I pointed out that was really not possible as my first loyalty was to Vickers-Armstrongs and in an emergency I could not have two bosses. But he disliked any other form of operation. As he said quite rightly, 'We shall not know where you are, and if we cannot warn you, you'll be shot to pieces before you can get off the ground.' Before we returned I was able to have a few words with David Atcherley, Catseyes Cunningham, Bats Page and several others whom I knew from peacetime, and who were now operational.

Up until that time we had been free of accidents and the routine, other than occasional trips to Eastleigh and Worthy Down, to assist Jeffrey with some development work, was uninterrupted. During November the weather had been unusually wet and I had been to Sywell to clear a Wellington. The aerodrome was in a terrible state with the grass churned up into large mudholes filled with water and whilst the Tiger Moths, which operated there, could avoid the worst of these holes, I had difficulty in doing so.

Having finished the Wellington I took off for Castle Bromwich in the Spitfire. Just as I was about to become airborne the wheels struck one of these large water-filled mudholes and the muddy mixture cascaded over the machine covering the front screen, but worst of all at about 50 ft the engine cut

* Later Air Vice-Marshal Sir Basil Embry.

completely. I couldn't turn right because of the Brooklands Aviation factory; I couldn't turn left because of the Tiger Moth hangars and the control tower; ahead was a small field and then a belt of trees in which stood a large manor house. I knew if I did not put the Spitfire down at once I would finish up in the trees or in the house, so with the chassis up and the flaps down I forced the belly of the machine onto the grass of this small field and we skated across the wet surface at a frightening speed. Just when I thought it would either plunge over onto its nose and turn onto its back or hit the trees with a God Almighty crack, the soft ground seemed to grab the underside like glue and we lurched to a standstill. Some Air Transport Auxiliary pilots taking delivery of the Wellington saw the whole thing and rushed over to me and helped carry my parachute back across the soggy field. As I could not afford to be delayed I told Bancroft I should have to borrow the Wellington I had just tested, to get me back to Castle Bromwich; such was the spirit of the time that he had it ready within minutes, with a crew all prepared to spend the night away.

Air Inspection Directorate inspectors were attached to each department, but were independent of any control by Vickers-Armstrongs personnel. In the main they did an excellent job under trying conditions and co-operated very well with our requirements. The procedure at that time was for the firm's inspectors to do a final inspection for flight and when completed this would be reported with the inspection papers for the head AID inspector to sign the form headed Air Ministry No. 1090, certifying that the machine was safe and ready for testing. On this particular occasion it was winter, cold and wet; it was Saturday afternoon and although we had not flown all that day, as was very often the case a string of machines appeared when it was almost too late to handle them. The whole atmosphere was miserable and depressing, particularly to me as a few days before my brother Eric had been killed in action. He had not reached his eighteenth birthday. I was fuming at the delay as the light was fading fast and I said to

Eric Holden, the firm's senior Flight Inspector, 'What the hell's
holding things up, Eric?' He replied, 'I really don't know; we
finished our inspection and the chits were handed in, but AID
have not given us the 1090s.' I said, 'Stir them up will you, or
we'll never get these cleared in this weather tonight.' He soon
came back to me and said, 'I'm sorry, Mr Henshaw, but the
chief AID inspector says he is not going to sign the 1090s
tonight, because in his opinion the weather is not good enough
to fly.' When I had recovered my breath I snarled, 'Flying has
nothing to do with AID. All I'm concerned with is that the
machines are ready for flight.' Eric replied, 'As far as we are
concerned, yes, but you can't fly them without the 1090.' I
stormed off to the little AID shed and opening the door said
to the chief AID inspector, 'My firm's inspector says these
machines are ready for flight, and that you will not sign the
1090s.' He replied in a somewhat supercilious manner. 'No,
it's getting late and in my opinion the weather is not suitable.'
I said, 'I'm the chief test pilot here. The responsibility for
weather and flying rests with me and has nothing whatever to
do with you. If you have not signed those 1090s in two minutes,
we shall fly without them.' He answered in a startled voice,
'You wouldn't dare.' I said, 'You just watch me.' I walked over
to George Snarey quickly and said, 'I've had a row with AID
and have told them I'm flying without a 1090. I know the
seriousness of this and what it may involve, so if you don't want
to fly I shall quite understand.' I then jumped into a machine
and took off and George followed me shortly afterwards. We
got all the machines up for the first time, but could not complete them as it was soon dark and the weather also worsened.

The following morning I was away and did the climb and
dive on one of the unfinished Spitfires on my way to Sywell,
where there was a Wellington awaiting me. I returned about
11 o'clock and as I taxied up to the RAF end of the Castle
Bromwich aerodrome I saw a group of senior staff from the
factory standing huddled together in deep discussion. It came
home to me at that moment that yesterday, whilst the AID

inspector had been wrong, I had also done something serious and unheard of and that I should have reported the incident to the chief of AID rather than have taken the action I had. I reflected I had never had the sack before, but in my present frame of mind I was not sorry. At least it saved me the responsibility of making a decision myself that neither Barbara nor Dad would have liked. As I climbed out of the cockpit Alex Dunbar and Mr Talamo came over to me. 'What's all the trouble with AID, Alex?' said Dunbar. I replied, 'I don't want to delve into details. Let's say there are two people on the aerodrome and there's really only room for one, and in any case I couldn't continue to work in an atmosphere like this.' Talamo who may not have been a dynamic General Manager, was nevertheless a gentleman and had a pacifying and charming manner. He said, 'Well, the AID man realises he has overstepped the mark and has assured us it will not happen again.' I said, 'I'm not looking for apologies. I've got a job to do and I'm going to do it. But as I said, I cannot work in this kind of atmosphere.' Alex Dunbar then chipped in, 'We've all got a job to do, if we are going to win this war. I've told Wickham to withdraw the inspector and you'll not see him again.' As far as I remember I never did, and we got on with things more quickly. Looking back it still strikes me as remarkable how long it took for an air of urgency to become general.

6 ✳ Bother, bombs and a balloon

THE BOMBING went on almost every night and sometimes during the day, but whatever the personal losses or griefs of the ordinary working people somehow they turned up to work and the job went on. The British people had their backs to the wall and if ever there were a finest hour in the history of the ordinary person, I think this was it.

I was brought back from a forced landing by a works car on 15 November and as we were near Coventry I told the driver to try and go through the city. It was the morning after the big raid by which the Germans extended their vocabulary with the word 'coventrate'. If I had not had my special pass we should not have been able to go through all the police barriers on the outskirts of the town; as it was we had to get out many times to find our way midst the burning, smoking rubble. I hope I never live to see a sight like it again: the Red Cross ambulances, the police and wardens with workers rushing in and out of the smouldering ruins, bringing out the dead and wounded. I pulled up next to a senior police officer, showed him my pass and said, 'It looks pretty bad.' He said, 'Yes, sir, it's about the worst we have had; they caught 1200 in that factory alone, and God knows how many more we are going to find when this lot's cleared up.'

Barbara and I, living in Hampton-in-Arden, were exactly in between Coventry and Birmingham, so it was rather unusual in those days for us to have an undisturbed night. If anyone tells me they liked the excitement of a bombing raid then I would say without hesitation, they want certifying. One night Jerry seemed to be bombing our house rather than Coventry or Birmingham and I rushed out into the courtyard to get hold of Tony my Labrador and bring him into the house; he was whimpering painfully and was as terrified as the rest of us. My little pet budgerigar died with the first blast and the noise and whistle of the bombs as they came down, with the retaliatory gunfire almost on our back door, was so overwhelming that Barbara was almost frozen to the spot, petrified and suffering uncontrolled trembling. I shouted above the din, 'Quick, the house is going! Let's get the car out and move further into the country.' As I ran the car out a bomb blasted the telephone post and I had difficulty in extricating the car from the tangled mass of wires, which fell down upon us.

In the morning when we could see, Barbara and I were both astonished to see so many buildings still standing, including our own house. The night previously I had left the Gull at Elmdon aerodrome, which was only a little over a mile down the road, so I cycled over to see if there was anything left. I could hardly see the aircraft for mud; a string of bombs had landed right across the Gull, one within twenty yards, but the ground was soft and the bomb had penetrated so deeply that it had merely pushed up a huge mound of clay and mud, partially covering the aircraft, but doing no other damage. I was able to clear this away and in another ten minutes had landed at Castle Bromwich where they had been more fortunate for once.

Alex Dunbar left the factory and his place as Managing Director was taken by Major Hew Kilner. Naturally enough with all the bombing the factory was having a very rough time and we had an unfortunate misunderstanding at the outset. I had met him a few months earlier when I had been over to Vickers-Armstrongs at their Blackpool works to fly the first Wellington production machine; I don't think he understood me and I always felt he thought I gave him less respect than a young employee should. The basic trouble was that the border-lines of authority had not been clearly marked out. We were all trying to do our best and we clashed in the way of going about it. It was a classic situation and not at all easy. We never had any harsh words, but there were times when I had to hold myself in check. The first of these was when my old friend, Wing Commander Thompson, was posted and his place taken over by Wing Commander Richard Kellett, a member of the RAF Wellesley long range team. I may have mentioned to him at some time or other that we should need another pilot but I was rather taken aback when Kellett rang me up one day and said, 'I've arranged for two service pilots to be posted to you and they are on their way.' I said as nicely as I could, 'Oh, that's very good of you, but I really don't need anyone just yet.' He replied, 'Well, it's all been arranged with Major Kilner that they are to come.' I replied that it had never been discussed and I could not see how he could know the flying requirements unless he spoke to me first.

A few months later we clashed again. This time Kilner opened by saying, 'It has been suggested that engines may be damaged by inverted flying during test trials.' Knowing that he was firing Kellett's bullets I said, 'Who suggests this?' Kilner looked at Kellett who said, 'Fighter Command are obviously anxious that no such damage should occur.' I replied, knowing very well what Kellett was getting at, 'I agree entirely with Fighter Command, but let us get the position straight: Spitfires are not flown inverted on test. It is true they are rolled and in certain cases an inverted glide takes place, but as the engine cuts immediately on negative "G", there is no power in use. I have discussed this at some length with the Rolls-Royce technicians and they are happy that no damage occurs.' Kellett said, 'It depends how long the machines remain inverted and what the revolutions are.' I answered, 'Agreed, but when I was at Eastleigh, both Jeffrey Quill and I were asked by AID to invert a Spitfire from 20,000 ft downwards in a series of trials, this was officially approved and as far as I know, no damage resulted from the tests.' I went on to both of them, 'I do my job to the best of my ability, and part of that job is to simulate any kind of flying conditions that may be encountered in combat. I'm not in the RAF; I'm not employed by the Ministry of Aircraft Production; Vickers-Armstrongs made my appointment to this factory and they can'—and here I looked straight at Major Kilner—'just as easily terminate that appointment if they so desire.' Kilner quickly came in and said, 'This is not under discussion, and I'm sure Wing Commander Kellett will be able to satisfy Fighter Command on the engine score.' I suggested that it would have been better, if there really had been a complaint, to put it through to me officially. The incident had the flavour of sour grapes. The meeting ended and from then on I got on quite well with Kilner. He never forgot it, however, for some years later when we were spending Christmas together he told our dinner guests humorously how I had once stood on my dignity and nearly walked out of his office.

In the early part of the war my job at Castle Bromwich was made more difficult because I really had no one in authority to whom I could appeal man-to-man when it came to a difficult decision. For instance, the towbar episode. My approach to the administration of the Flight Shed was to make everything we did as simple and as inexpensive as possible. In fact I treated everything I did during this period with Vickers-Armstrongs as if it was my own organisation and I was spending my own money. I knew that soon we were going to handle large numbers of aircraft, so that the first thing we really needed was a number of small, compact manoeuvrable tractors with a suitable light towbar that could be operated easily. In conjunction with the Works Manager I had them design and construct a very simple towbar, which could be operated by one man. One day early in 1940, however, the Works Manager rang me up and said, 'What do you want to do with the first of these towing bogies?' When I asked him what he meant he said, 'These four-wheel bogies that someone's designed and they've told me to make. It needs four men to lift the machine into position. I think they'll be all right as long as the tractor does not go over rough ground, but then there's a possibility that the prop might get damaged.' 'How much are they costing?' I asked, 'and how many have been ordered?' He answered, 'Well, we've spent about £50 on this one so far and we have another forty-nine to make.' I said, 'Well, I've no jurisdiction in the matter, but I can tell you here and now that we shall certainly not use them and I suggest you get through to the source that ordered them and tell them so.' No more was heard of the bogies. Our towbar proved to be so economical and satisfactory that we used them throughout the war years without any modifications, and I think the cost was £6 each.

Some while later I left my large, noisy, dull office in the main assembly block and moved over to the spacious, light and in many respects, eminently suitable office just completed, over at the Flight Shed. Flight Shed is really too humble a word to use for these buildings, which were to be my working home for so many of those long years. They were really three enormous factory blocks, and I would think probably the finest establishment of their kind you would find anywhere. I liked my office, but before my Managing Director of that time, B. W. A. Dickson, of whom much more later, saw the effect it was having on me and ordered it to be soundproofed and double-glazed, it was dreadfully noisy; many times as the engines were run up on the hangar apron the glass pen and pencil holders we had at the time would shatter on the desk into a hundred pieces as the sound frequency produced by the Merlins reached a crescendo and vibrated the glass to destruction.

In front of my new office and serving as a gigantic apron to the three Flight Shed blocks, was an enormous expanse of reinforced concrete, clean and neatly laid with finishing touches of camouflage paint barely dry. One morning the Works Manager came over with men, pneumatic drills, concrete mixer and the whole paraphernalia and asked where he was to dig up the concrete to put in some enormous petrol tanks. I was getting a little used to this by now so I said, 'You're not going to dig up this concrete if I can help it. You will have to put the tanks somewhere else.' He answered, 'I can't do this; we have to work to these plans'—which he had in his hands. I dug my heels in and said, 'Well, you can do what you like, but I'm not going to allow you to hack up this concrete. You had better go back to the factory and sort it out.' When he returned he was all smiles and said, 'I've seen Mr Talamo and I have to put the tanks where you think best.' We went to look at the side of the building, where there was no concrete, and that is where the tanks were put. The only concrete to be touched was the new mixture which was put over the tanks after installation.

The Air Transport Auxiliary were responsible for clearance of all tested aircraft from the factory. Most were private pre-war pilots who had been unable to join the Services for one reason or another and many were women pilots of considerable experience, some of whom I had known for many years. For obvious reasons they disliked clearing machines from Castle Bromwich and I was very amused recently to read in the very excellent book on the history of the ATA by Miss Lettice Curtis that the 'hot' boys would go into Castle Bromwich and when the balloons were up close on three sides of the airfield, with the wind necessitating a take-off towards them, they would emulate the Chief Test Pilot by a roll off a half-loop from the ground, which would put them on their way clear of the lethal cables. It is a good story, but I am quite sure that Miss Curtis never saw this actually happen, for I never did. When I wanted to take-off under those conditions I went off down wind, which was far less trouble.

Flight Lieutenant L. D. Wilson was the first service pilot attached to me. He had a permanent commission and on the whole it worked out quite well. We found Wilson most useful when during the bad weather, machines accumulated before the ATA had collected them and I thought they were too much of a risk to remain on the aerodrome and decided we would deliver them ourselves to the various units. Wilson would usually fly a Blenheim and George Snarey and I Spitfires. It was slow and tedious, but then at that time we did not have a very great production.

Once I borrowed a Dragon from the RAF at Castle Bromwich complete with a very experienced Polish pilot and we were very busy moving for a day or so. The pilot had done 8000 hours but nevertheless when we had delivered the machines I flew the Dragon back with a full load of pilots. On the last flight of the day, however, I said to the Polish pilot as he had worked so well, 'I'm sorry I've taken over from you every time; perhaps you would like to fly us back.' He took it as I had intended—a compliment to his ability and I joined the other pilots in the passenger seats. We were all a bit tired so there was not much conversation and I nodded off in a doze. About an hour later I heard a gasp from the pilot next to me and he shook my shoulder pointing frantically out of the side window, I sprang to life and just saw a balloon cable disappearing into the gloom as the light began to fade. Rushing up to the small single-seat cockpit I literally dragged the startled Pole out while the Dragon floated around with no one at the controls for a few moments, until I was able to squeeze into position to take over. I realised at once that we must have hit the outskirts of Birmingham too far to the west and were now well in amongst the balloon defence barrage. I pushed the nose of the Dragon literally onto the tops of the houses so that I might see the balloon hoists before we ran into the cables. Then I reasoned that there would not be a hoist on a main road, so the first likely looking road I saw running southwards I clung to like a leech with all my pilots in the back shouting encouragement and keeping a sharp lookout. Once we had left the built-up area I knew we were safe and swinging eastwards and then north we were not long picking up the familiar landmarks around Castle Bromwich.

We were all issued with gas masks and steel helmets as a matter of course, but for a long while I never carried my tin hat around with me; one, because it was cumbersome, and two, because I could never fly with it. One day in the late afternoon, just before we had moved over to our new Flight Shed we had about twenty machines clustered together awaiting flight trials or having adjustments, when a Junkers 88 came out of the low, dark stratus cloud to the east of the factory and passing right

over the airfield disappeared into the cloud again. I yelled out
to everyone around me, 'That's a dummy run, disperse the
machines quickly!' I grabbed a tractor, pushing out of the way
our old driver Tom, tore across the airfield and dumped a
Spitfire. When I rushed back for another one, this time Tom
was ready for me and hitching on another machine we tore
out again. We were just about to unhitch when I saw the 88
break cloud in almost the same place as before, and I could not
help a tinge of admiration going through me for the pilot, as
the base of the cloud was only about 400–500 ft. The bomb
doors swung open and I marvelled at the pilot's audacity as he
slowly approached, juggling the machine as he did so, rather
like a hen about to settle on a clutch of eggs. All hell was let
loose as the defences came into action and the show was a good
deal better than many firework displays. The Junkers 88
seemed unperturbed and ignoring all the shells and tracer,
prepared to drop its bombs. It came over me with a shock that
I was dead in line and my mouth went dry as a huge bomb
left the machine gracefully, and plunged towards us. I yelled
to Tom, who was in any case touching me, 'I reckon this is
addressed to us, Tom,' and we both buried our faces in the
ground. The bomb, however, sailed over the top of us and hit
a small house on the edge of the aerodrome, about fifty yards
from all the machines, injuring two of my Flight Shed men who
were there. All the men did their job well and not a single
machine was damaged. Some officials from the factory and
some AID inspectors jumped into a slit-trench nearby when the
bomb was dropped and to our amusement there had been
heavy rain that day and the trench was almost full to the brim
with water. As Tom and I crouched by the tractor a piece of
shrapnel from somewhere hit the ground almost at my feet
with such a thud that it sprayed mud everywhere. From then
on I carried my tin hat constantly.

Visits to the factory by important individuals were now
almost a constant feature. Mrs Churchill, for instance, visited
the factory several times on her own before she came later on

with the Prime Minister. The first important official visit by H.M. King George VI was not well organised. I was sent briefing instructions, set out in great detail: I was to be presented near my office in the assembly block; there was to be no visit by His Majesty to the aerodrome and none of the other Flight Shed personnel or pilots were to be presented. I spoke to Talamo about this as my first reaction was not to attend either, and to remain on the aerodrome. When I saw him he was obviously worried about the visit and although he agreed he said he could not possibly ask the directors to alter the schedule now; they had spent hours with officials from all over the place going over every detail and as His Majesty had so little time to spare only selected people were to be presented. They thought it would be a good idea, though, if after I had been presented I could fly over the factory before His Majesty left. The whole thing was rather sad; the King spoke a few words to me, but he looked tired and depressed. When I flew over the factory he was inside one of the blocks; he saw none of the flying and all that I achieved was to interrupt noisily other presentations still going on.

Almost each day the war news became worse, and as it did so I felt obliged to make more strenuous efforts to pull my weight. I was now responsible for the expenditure of hundreds of thousands of gallons of fuel, so as I knew people thought I had petrol to burn I decided to cycle to and from work, which was about five miles away. I think many thought it was 'not quite the thing' for someone of my status to arrive in flying overalls and on a bicycle, but I didn't give it a thought. It kept me fit and it set an example to those who knew I had not only unlimited use of petrol, but of aircraft as well. In any case the quiet cycle ride gave me the opportunity to think without interruption. My brother Leslie had been persuaded out of being a rear-gunner and was now in the thick of the fighting in the Western Desert; as a driver in the 13th Light Field Ambulance, he was soon to be on his way to the Far East.

Quite soon both Kellett and Kilner were moved on elsewhere

and for the first time I made the acquaintance of B. W. A. Dickson, the new Managing Director. Dickson knew nothing about aircraft but he had had a great deal of factory experience with Vickers-Armstrongs. I liked him at once and when we understood one another we became very firm friends; in fact closer, and I think that the relationship was almost that of father and son. Dick really made Castle Bromwich tick; he knew his job and I knew I could rely upon him. I think, with all due modesty, that he thought he could rely on me. Dorrie, his wife, was a wonderful person, so full of vigour and vitality that she sometimes left Barbara and me breathless.

Kellett's place was taken by Wing Commander Becker. Bernard Becker was a nice person and was to be the Castle Bromwich RAF overseer for a longer period than any other officer; he was always helpful and we got on well the whole of the time he was there. Wilson was posted that spring and his place taken by Flight Lieutenant Sanders. Sandy, as he became known, was a bright young fighter pilot, recently returned from a hot operational tour in Malta. He was a good, clean boy and did his job well.

About this time, whereas before I had never given much thought to the question of survival at my job, I now began to be aware that accidents were happening with regularity and frequency. The area over which we flew was not the most encouraging for forced landings to say the least; also with the frantic production pressures on everywhere, one was not too sure of other factors connected either with the airframe or the engine. When Sanders was late from a test flight one day I put out an overdue signal. I was distressed when I was quickly given the news that his machine had broken up in the air and that only a mangled lump of bloody flesh and bones remained of poor old Sandy. I began to wonder what would happen as the pressures grew, for at the moment the outlook could not have been worse.

I had just had a forced landing, which had shaken me although I was completely untouched. During a take-off westwards over the factory the engine cut just as I was over the boundary of the airfield. If I had followed the unbreakable rule never to turn down wind on engine failure but keep straight on, I should have landed on top of Dunlops or our own factory, so I pushed the nose down quickly as I turned back, losing height so rapidly that if the old Castle Bromwich Clubhouse roof had been a foot higher I should not have made it. I flicked the emergency landing gear lever downwards but the margins were so fine, and it had happened with such suddenness, with the machine almost dropping onto the ground downwind, that only one leg of the chassis locked into position. As the machine rocketed over the grass, I felt the port leg start to fold up and the wing first scraped and then dug into the soft ground; spinning round we jerked to an abrupt halt. I suppose to those watching it was just a neat piece of flying, other than the chassis collapsing, but only I knew how close it had been before I appeared stepping calmly from the cockpit; I paused to offer a silent prayer of thanks. During the investigation a large split-pin was found in the magneto distributor housing; this could only have been sabotage at the point of assembly, as no such type of split-pins were used on the whole magneto, and before that cover was bolted up it must have been subject to a very close and careful examination. We had heard all sorts of rumours about incidents with torches and rockets at night and also sabotage to certain engines being found in flight, but I had not believed them and thought the stories exaggerated. I knew most of my own men extremely well by now, but of course we were taking on increasing numbers and these were complete strangers. There were those like Bill Buckley, Eric Holden and Jim Hastings, whom I would have trusted with my life, but this isolated incident caused us to look at one another and wonder if these newcomers could really be trusted. There was nothing I could really do about it, but I went over to the Home Guard armoury and told the man in charge to show me where I could grab a loaded rifle in a hurry, if I wanted it.

Some of the incidents were almost inexplicable. One frantic Saturday we were inundated with the usual rush of 'last minute' production quotas and had nearly twenty machines to get into the air. Suddenly Eric Holden and Munro the Senior AID Inspector rushed over to my office and said all machines must be grounded at once. Apparently on final assembly the inspector had noticed that the honing on the main spar where it bolted on to the fuselage lacked its usual polish. Puzzled, he called for a hardness test of the spar metal and it was found that none of the recent batch of spars had been through the special hardness treatment and that in the present state they had a safety factor of about 3 to 4. I reckoned on that Saturday morning we could have had five or six pilots up in the air at the same time and that most of them would put on a 'G' load of at least 6 or 7.

Sandy's remains were cremated near his home town, a wretched day for a sad occasion. The only thing that brought a shade of relief to the sombre surroundings for me was when I saw the look of consternation on Bernard Becker's face as he watched the large Union Jack over the coffin disappear smoothly and silently through the oak door hatch into the cubicle for cremation. I guessed immediately his thoughts: he was in charge of the flag and he assumed at the time that it would be burnt and he would have to account for it.

With Cosford, Desford, Cowley, Sywell and Castle Bromwich to cover, all building up to increased production, I had started taking on more pilots. In addition I was involved with conferences from time to time with the RAF personnel, either at Boscombe Down or Castle Bromwich, or meetings at the factory or at Supermarines at Hursley Park and also development work at Worthy Down, where Jeffrey Quill had now moved after the bombing of Eastleigh, and I kept in touch as often as conditions would permit. I went back to Eastleigh airfield for the last time on a very sad occasion, to say a final farewell to George Pickering. He was buried in a little churchyard near where he had flown for so long. His death was a tragic accident; as I recollect he had had a forced landing and was hurt, so he went to the West Country to recuperate and whilst out on a walk was given a lift in an army Bren Gun carrier. The carrier was attempting a steep gradient when it toppled over; George was thrown out and killed instantly. As we stood in silent prayer, I was reminded of the last fatal accident I had seen at Eastleigh, within yards of where we stood at that moment. I had finished flying and had taken off my overalls and as it was sunny I was watching a Skua about to take off. Although it was a nice day the wind was strong and gusty, but as I watched I did not feel this as I was sheltered by the office buildings. The Skua moved off slowly with the usual tail-down technique and when at just about flying speed it suddenly lurched into the sky and flicked over onto its back. Without hesitation I grabbed a fire extinguisher from the office wall and ran as I have never run before, thinking that the pilot would be swearing at his clumsiness and praying that the machine would not go up in smoke before we got to him or he got out. Running with a large cylinder is no joke and as I gasped my way nearer to use the extinguisher, I was stopped in my tracks with horror. There was no smoke or fire but a few yards in front of me was a mangled human head and a little further away underneath a comparatively undamaged Skua was the rest of the torso. As the machine had flicked over into the ground it had obviously scrubbed the top decking away killing the occupants instantly. As there had been nothing I could do I had allowed the clanging fire tender and ambulance to shoot past me and slowly and sickly walked back to the office.

7 ✳ *A Tomtit in the garden*

WITH THE WEATHER improving, the Gull was put to such good use that I realised that we ought to have another machine, and when three Tomtits from the Leicestershire Aero Club were advertised for sale I went over and bought them. First built as a trainer in the late 1920s the Hawker Tomtit stayed in service with the RAF until 1935, when they were put up for sale to private buyers. They were slow, manoeuvrable machines that were really unsuitable in some ways, but they had the advantage that they would take off and land on the proverbial postage stamp. I also had in mind that the times when I was rushed, I could land in the small field that adjoined the paddock at The Ridings and I could be from home to work in less than five minutes if need be. We flew two of the Tomtits back and the RAF delivered the unassembled third machine on one of their Queen Marys. I had gone over by car and had forgotten to take my goggles; when I landed at Castle Bromwich my eyes were filled with water and I did a nice bounce in the middle of the airfield, much to the amusement of the onlookers. I later sold one of these Tomtits to Jeffrey Quill and he flew it for many years. The others were in use constantly, Vickers-Armstrongs doing the servicing and repairs, which I thought at the time a fair exchange considering they were flown only on company business. One still remains intact to this day and flies at meetings as a vintage aircraft for the Shuttleworth aviation museum at Old Warden.

Early in 1941 production at Castle Bromwich changed over to the Spitfire Mark V. In appearance it was almost identical with the Mark I or Mark II when fitted with the 'A' type wing. When fitted with the 'B' wing it had two 20 mm cannon and four ·303 machine-guns; with the 'C' wing four 20 mm cannons only; and for the 'D' wing there was the combination of two 20 mm cannons and two ·5 machine-guns. The empennage and nose had not changed in shape except on the tropicalised version, which had a snub-nosed appearance due to the large intake filter which spoiled its otherwise clean profile. The camouflage paint scheme had also not altered, except again, on the tropicalised version—they were painted a light brown and sandy yellow which after the drabness, to which we had now long been accustomed, looked to our war-weary eyes almost festive. With the various modifications that had been creeping in, such as improved armour-plating, self-sealing tanks and heavier guns and ammunition, etc., the gross weight had now reached almost 1000 lb more than the first Spitfire I had flown at Eastleigh. We were fitting the Merlin 45 which gave another 10–12 mph in maximum speed at 20,000 ft and we could now reach 25,000 ft in the same time that the Mark I took to reach slightly under 20,000 ft. The Mark V came out in several guises but the one I enjoyed most of all was the model fitted with the Merlin 50M engine, and the 'A' type wing. This was a cropped blower or de-rated engine, designed to give its maximum power at 5500 ft. It had of course a big advantage at low level and with the enormous increase in boost pressure, it was a joy to fly. In fact it was the only Spitfire during a demonstration that I felt able to take-off, lift the wheels up, pause and then pull up firmly but smoothly into a vertical loop with a slow-roll off the top to finish over the centre of the airfield. If I had to make a choice of all the numerous marks of Spitfires—and there were over thirty-six of them—this is the one I would have picked for a low-level display.

I found myself in some difficulty at group conferences at times, particularly when held at Hursley Park. My loyalty was to Castle Bromwich and if some high-ranking outside official or RAF officer said something with which I did not agree, I would soon make my own opinions known. It was at times like this that I realised the value of being a civilian when talking to very senior officers in uniform as I was not subject to their service protocol. With members of Supermarines, however, it was different, because they were nearly all old friends, so that when the Castle Bromwich RTO went out to have sharp words with Joe Elliott or Mansbridge, I found myself silently agreeing with the Supermarine people. The only time I used to dig my heels in against Supermarines was when I was asked to do development work with the Castle Bromwich production machines. I pointed out that I was more than willing to conduct any trials but they must provide the aircraft, because the only thing that really mattered to the Castle Bromwich management was production and this could not be delayed or interfered with under any circumstances.

Sometimes we had a contentious matter to settle, which involved Castle Bromwich, Supermarine, the Fleet Air Arm and the RAF. One such occasion was when the basic setting of some new de Havilland V/P airscrews were suspect by Fighter Command and it had been reported that it was possible to over-rev the engine in a power dive. To alter the pitch setting meant a slightly impaired take-off and when told by the RAF that the engine revs would go off the clock in a maximum power dive, I said I did not believe it: they would go to the maximum permitted revs per minute but no more. The outcome was that I was to conduct the trials myself and deliver the machines to Boscombe Down for the RAF test pilot to do the same. I was a bit rattled over this business, not because it was suggested that the basic pitch setting should be altered, but because an RAF pilot implied that he knew more about diving Spitfires than I did.

The first series of trials only confirmed what I already knew: there was a reasonable safety margin when dived at any height with full power. I then decided I would dive the machine to its utmost terminal velocity speed. I climbed to about 37,000 ft and pushed the nose over in a vertical dive. This was not really successful as the engine cut in the early stages if I applied too much negative 'G' and if I kept the engine in power the angle of the dive was not steep enough. In the final dive I did a level run at 37,000 ft for some few minutes and then half rolled straight into a vertical dive; the technical department at Castle Bromwich had not been able to provide me with a calibrated ASI so I shall never know the exact speed in that particular dive. On the ASI I was able to read off at between 560 and 570 IAS and the revs did in fact go 100 over the maximum permissible, but this took place at only one critical phase. At high altitude obviously the power output of the engine was reduced in the rarified air and lower down when the power did come in, with the denser air this kept the engine revs down. In plotting the two curves it was where these two lines crossed that was the critical point. The interesting thing about the test was that the ailerons, as expected, went rock solid at about 400–450 IAS onwards and then the elevators; I had taken the somewhat puerile precaution of not fastening my safety harness so that if the machine broke up I might stand a chance of being thrown clear; but lacking the comforting feel of the shoulder straps I felt as if I were almost naked. As the Spitfire hurtled earthwards with the controls rigid, when I put some pressure on the control column it moved me easily from my seat at the angle I sat. The utmost delicacy was needed to ease the machine out at that speed and as I could not pull the control column back, I used the trimmer tab as if it were as fragile as a biscuit. The machine pulled out quite easily and I felt more relieved and certainly happier than I had been before.

At the conference at Boscombe Down I was able to voice my opinion with confidence and the meeting went off extremely well, particularly when I found myself discussing the position with a very able senior ranking technician. He had reached the same conclusion in plotting the rev curves as myself. Whilst over-revving would never normally occur it was better to play safe, and the basic setting was altered slightly.

On some of the tropicalised Spitfires with Rotol airscrews fitted we had an engine rev problem of a different nature. These airscrews had the pitch range but they suffered with control-valve trouble which caused the airscrew to stick in fine pitch if the throttle was snapped back in a steep climb and then snapped open again as the machine dived. This happened to one of my service pilots, Lieutenant Jack Shepherd, on the first occasion and although I was at home working in the garden, I heard the screaming crescendo as if it was right over me. No further damage was done other than the necessity to have the engine changed. I had difficulty in getting action to remedy this defect from the manufacturers as that was the first time they had heard of it, but in the end they confirmed that all the airscrews would be modified at the Maintenance Units before delivery to the squadrons. Later these same Spitfires were in action against the Japs and flown by Australian pilots and in one action so many Australians were lost that I sincerely hoped to God the airscrews had not been responsible for this disaster.

In the course of my years at Castle Bromwich and the many hundreds of demonstrations that took place, I only remember one important one when the flying was badly disrupted because of weather. This happened to be one of Dick Dickson's first organised meetings of importance, when press representatives from the news media throughout the whole Allied world came to see and write up Castle Bromwich as the most important factory of its kind this side of the Atlantic. He had briefed me and I was anxious to put on a good show. I was going to lead a flight of three Spitfires in close formation in a series of manoeuvres over and around the airfield and would finish up with my usual display. On the actual day, however, we were all despondent to find the weather was hopeless, with fog reducing visibility to about 200 yards. From my office we watched the long stream of gleaming cars move slowly from the factory, enter the airfield near the RAF Admin. Block and continue like a long black caterpillar on the narrow road which served for towing the Spitfires over for test and which also provided a convenient take-off runway for us. Dick came over to me as the large party pulled up and with a grimace said, 'What rotten luck, Alex; the only thing they really wanted to see was the flying.' When they had been shown around our quarters, Dick said to me on the side, 'There's no chance of any flying, is there?' I replied, 'Not really. I can take a machine up but I'm afraid they won't see much.' 'I think they'll be satisfied with anything,' he said, so I offered to trickle one round the field for them to see how slowly the Spit could fly. I took off down the towing strip at the feet of the journalists and of course was lost to sight almost immediately. By keeping the boundary of the aerodrome in sight I knew when to turn off to fly in front of the Flight Sheds and with wheels up and flaps down I trickled past the small crowd at stalling speed to disappear again out of sight. I did this several times with flaps and wheels up and again down, then following the familiar landmarks on and around the airfield I did one or two faster low vertical turns so that they would get an impression of the manoeuvrability and control and then as the large black hangars, with the white faces of the visitors enabled me to use them as an orientation point, I did one slow roll in front of them to the south and turning out of sight came in to do another one to the north. It is easier to roll accurately fast than it is to do it at slow speed but I dare not build up too much speed, as although the hangars were large, once I had passed them by out of the roll, I could not see any horizon. The grey grass of the ground was merging into the fog so that it was not easy to see at all.

When I landed I was surprised to see how jubilant Dick was. 'You've pulled it right out of the bag,' he exclaimed. Certainly it had livened up a dull party and they were now shooting questions right, left and centre. It was some time before they got into their cars and left.

A little later, at another demonstration I was having a friendly chat to the then Parliamentary Private Secretary to the Minister for Air, when he said, 'You saved the day for us when all those press people came down and I personally am very grateful; but, and I ought not to tell you this, you were reported for dangerous flying to the Minister.' I was a bit shaken by this and asked, 'Who would do a thing like that, and what on earth for?' The PPS went on, 'It's someone you know. When he sent in a written report it coincided with several other letters on the same subject but all praising the whole visit and in particular the flying that was put on for them in such conditions. We had to deal with this complaint officially of course, and I recommended to the Minister that this report either be substantiated or withdrawn, and if neither was done we would ask for his special Air Ministry pass to be returned.' I thanked the PPS for his support and wondered who had done it. I had an idea it must have been someone who could fly and knew something about flying and I only knew of one press representative at that meeting who flew. But I never really found out who it was.

I never had time to visit old friends, but occasionally they were able to call upon me. Brian Field came in one day; he had once tried to persuade me to go in with him on a world speed record attempt. He was now testing aircraft with the Miles Aircraft Company. When we had chatted a while he said, 'Alex, when you test repaired machines at Cowley, do you treat them the same as a new aircraft?' I replied, 'Well, yes; after all they go back to squadrons in most cases and if they have not the performance of a new aircraft our job is to find out the reason why.' He then asked about the dive, 'Do you reduce the speed of this?' I answered, 'No, every repaired Spitfire that I have flown has exactly the same treatment as a new machine.' 'I'm glad to hear this,' he went on, 'because I have been involved with some strong arguments recently that a used aircraft cannot be expected to stand up to the same stresses as a new one, and you have confirmed my own feelings.' Brian went back and bearing in mind the type of machine he was testing, I wondered for a second or so whether my advice to him had been sound. I suddenly remembered that once when I was talking to Jeffrey at Eastleigh as we stood on the airfield in May of 1940, there before our eyes we saw a piece of material fly off a Miles Master that was going by in the distance, and the machine suddenly plunged into what was known as Fisher's Pond. As we arrived the police were still probing for the pilot.

I had forgotten about Brian's visit until one day I was in my usual hurry, and as the Tomtit was not an easy machine to start I asked a firm's inspector nearby to nip into the cockpit and operate the switches and throttle. The machine took several turns of the prop but did not start. I swung back the propeller to clear the engine and then shouted to the inspector, 'Contact'. The engine burst into life at full throttle and I stepped smartly aside as the machine came forward, expecting that the inspector would close the throttle and step down from the cockpit. When I glanced towards him, however, his hair was standing on end with the slipstream, he was clutching the sides of the cockpit rigidly with both hands and his mouth was wide open yelling blue murder with fear. I was splitting my sides with laughter and being tempted very much to let the machine go. In the end I dug one of my heels firmly into the ground as I hung onto a wingtip and the Tomtit lifted its tail to come down with a dreadful crunch with pieces of the wooden propeller flying all over the place. By this time all the Flight Shed personnel had arrived on the scene and as Eric Holden came up to me I shouted, 'For God's sake get that silly bastard out of my sight, Eric; if I get near him I'll break his bloody neck.' There were screams of laughter because as I said this the terrified inspector was running very distressed into the seclusion of the hangar. Luckily the only damage sustained was a broken propeller, which I knew I should be able to get from Brian Field.

After Eric Holden had given me the diameter and pitch of the airscrew required I rang Brian Field's office. I knew in his private capacity as an aircraft spares dealer he would most probably have one of the right type in stock. After some delay I was put through to his secretary. She sounded most distressed and then said, 'I'm terribly sorry, Mr Henshaw; I know you were a great friend of Mr Field's, but he was killed yesterday in an air crash.' I started to ask what had happened, but she broke down and I had to ring off. I then had a word with Tommy Rose who also worked for the Miles Aircraft Company. 'Well, you know as well as I, Alex, Brian was a pretty thorough chap and some of these repaired machines take a bit of hammering. He would insist on diving them like a new machine. We're not sure what happened yet, but the first reports indicate that something came adrift.'

The stresses on aircraft today are widely researched and more is known than in my early days, where often we groped a little in the dark. When we made a determined effort to achieve the fastest speed in the King's Cup Race of 1938, I was vaguely aware of the gyroscopic loads on the airframe and engine during high-speed turns but no one had been able to give me an analysis with conviction of what the combination of speed, positive 'G' and the untested leverage forces would do to the crankshaft, if not to the airframe. When I first flew a Spitfire at over 40,000 ft with similar gyroscopic problems due to the flexibility of the airscrew blades, had I not been strapped in I should have been thrown through the cockpit roof. Experience testing my modified Mew Gull in the '30s had prepared me for it.

Nevertheless, whilst we knew very little by today's standards, there were many very obvious ways overstressing of engine or airframe could be checked. Those who think a test pilot's job is to test an aircraft to near destruction probably have been watching Hollywood films: this of course is sheer nonsense, particularly in wartime production testing. Here the job of the pilot is to test within design limitations and for a specific purpose: to prove that each completed aircraft conforms to the previously approved and tested design and is 100 per cent sound and suitable to be handed over for active service. If a production aircraft were overstressed during the process, it would, I think, be a very serious reflection upon the test pilot concerned.

Certainly there are exceptions and borderline cases, such as an engine being over-revved because of a faulty airscrew constant-speed valve. Again, on the early Mark 21, when we were told by the design office to dive to 520 IAS, occasionally this dive overstressed the cooling duct and fairing over the glycol radiators and they tore away from the airframe. The fairing was then modified and I remember the design office at the same time limiting future dives to 500 IAS.

Our complete life now hinged around the job with Vickers-Armstrongs; hours, nights and days ceased to count any more. Sunday was just another day, depending whether I was on duty or off; if I was off it would be spent in the garden. The grounds of The Ridings were laid out by a landscape gardener. Unfortunately, our own gardener had left and if Barbara had not helped me, we certainly could not have kept the garden and lawns in the immaculate condition we both loved to see. In addition the food shortage was now being felt and we made a determined effort to create a large kitchen garden that would make us self-sufficient. I had never gardened before but by the time we had finished, not only were we able to produce nearly all our own vegetables, but our strawberries were some of the finest we had ever eaten. During the first summer at Hampton-in-Arden the grass in our little paddock grew to nearly waist height and I wore myself out cutting it with a scythe. Neither did my temper improve when I had to burn the hay as no one wanted it. Determined to make better use of the ground we decided that winter to plant an orchard. When I came to plant the trees, however, I found myself digging in solid clay and realised I must thoroughly drain the whole paddock if I was to have any success with our fruit-trees. All this took time and effort but in the end we could almost feed ourselves winter and summer, particularly with the ducks and chickens. In retrospect, I suppose it was, for me, hard physical work and with the sweat I worked out of my system I retained sanity, away from the daily demanding grind, in the comparative peace of the Warwickshire countryside.

My practice was to be on call wherever I was and no aircraft was to be kept waiting for flight trials if it was possible to be

Above, left Jeffrey Quill, *right* Mutt Summers
Below Jicha and A.H. ready for firewatching

Above Aerial view of the Works, Castle Bromwich
Below Undercarriage test rig

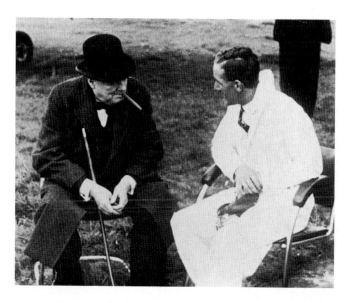

Above Winston Churchill and A.H.
Below Barbara and Alex Jun.

Farewell, Spitfire! A Mark 22 above the clouds

avoided. This sometimes brought on its own troubles. We now had good AID inspectors in the Flight Shed, who understood me and fitted into our working programme willingly. Munro, the senior inspector, came to me when I said that Hastings would have a night shift going and that we would start flying at first light. In June, of course, that was around 3.30 to 4 o'clock in the morning, and he said in his Scots accent, 'You know, Mr Henshaw, I'm a wee bit troubled. Our men are only allowed to work so many hours a week. I've let the odd week over-run but then I have to make our monthly returns and I can see I'm going to be well over my allotted schedule, and I canna do this, and if I do I shall have the head office on my back.' I said laughingly, 'Oh dear, oh dear, this really is serious. I should get through to head office and ask them to hold the war up a bit, until we can catch up.' And then seriously I said, 'Mr Munro, I've got my job to do, you've got yours. All I can tell you is if those machines are ready, we are going to fly them. So I'm afraid you had better get through to your head office and tell them so.'

Cullum at Cowley had said on more than one occasion I could send a pilot over any time, day or night if they had a machine ready for test. The first time I told them I would be over early was about 4 o'clock in the morning and to my annoyance when I arrived the airfield had anti-invasion poles stuck up all over the airfield. These were elaborate steel girders which were hinged into concrete bases and when necessary could be pulled into the upright position and could be kept there by locking pins. When not in use they could then be folded down level with the ground, and were so good that I had not really noticed them on landings there before. I circled low and was just about to go on to Sywell, where I knew there was a Wellington ready for test, when the devil in me said, 'I wonder what they would say about their precious defences if I landed a Spitfire in between them.' Looking at them carefully from the air I could see how the steel poles lined up and with a little manoeuvring I was sure I could land safely without touching them. This I did, and as I turned around the last lane to come up to the factory apron, men were rushing around everywhere in a frantic chase to unlock and fold away the steel girders. Cullum came up and with a shocked look on his face said, 'I daren't tell you how much we spent on those anti-invasion defences; and to think we were assured by the experts that not even a Tiger Moth would be able to land.'

Those June days were long and if I could not have used the Tomtit from my back garden, they would have been even longer. As it was, some days were from 3 o'clock in the morning until 12 at night and needless to say I needed no rocking to sleep.

War or no war, factories were going to have their holidays, so Barbara and I decided we would take advantage of this and visit Ireland, where her sister lived. To go by train and boat was almost impossible so I asked Jeffrey Quill if he would loan me Supermarine's newly acquired twin-engined Dragonfly and I would put in an official appearance at Shorts at Belfast. The break did us both the world of good and we spent most of the time swimming and fishing on the almost deserted beaches around Giant's Causeway and Portrush. I was recognised only once, by an Irishman who was staying with his family in the same hotel, and some weeks later at home, I received the most gigantic and elaborate box of assorted chewing gums I had ever seen. Inside on a card it said, 'American Friends Overseas. Mr MacDonell has sent your name at our request as the most deserving man he knows to receive our monthly jumbo present to our friends across the water.' I brought Jeffrey back a beautiful salmon, caught the same morning, but it was such a hot day that as I spoke to him on our return to Worthy Down, the smell of stinking fish wafted across the aerodrome to such an extent that the gift assumed dubious proportions.

Later that year I was delighted to be informed that my request for gunned-up Spitfires for factory defence had been granted and that two machines would be delivered to me by

Fighter Command. The next step was to get some gunnery practice, so I asked Wing Commander Becker if he would organise this for me at an OTU. There was a snag at once: I was told I could not shoot a German if I was wearing civilian clothes; I should be classed as a spy or a *franc-tireur*. Beaverbrook had the bright idea that as a civilian I should wear the armband of a Sergeant Pilot. This suited me, although all I wanted to do was to shoot Germans if I had the chance. As long as they were dead I reasoned that they wouldn't really be in a position to argue, whether I had a uniform on or not. It did not end there, however. When Becker made the arrangements at the Operational Training Unit at Hawarden, according to my rank I should have to go into the Sergeants' Mess. The last time I had been to Hawarden I had been accorded VIP treatment; my status in war or peace was such that it would have been perfectly normal for me to have sat in the Mess with the Commanding Officer, so that they were a little embarrassed at this stage as to the correct procedure. I solved the problem for all concerned by saying that I would not stay in a Mess but would travel to and fro from Castle Bromwich each day; this worked out very well in spite of odd remarks that I should be late for the courses. As the Tomtit was too slow I borrowed a Sparrowhawk. I set off bright and early each day to be taught how to shoot.

Once I had mastered the radio telephony jargon and code the rest was comparatively easy. The only real thing I wanted was practice; to reduce wastage only two guns were loaded during target practice, which was carried out on the range along the Flintshire coast. The first time I went onto the range there was a strong cross wind and it was bumpy and I could not see where my bullets were striking. On the third run in as I opened up to pull away from the firing range, the engine cut and I automatically set the machine up to land on the beach, as I did so it cut in again and after a cautious climb I returned to Hawarden, got hold of the Flight Sergeant who serviced the machine and told him what had happened, saying that I suspected a fuel stoppage. The course carried on and I enjoyed the change. On the fifth day the Commanding Officer was asking me how I was getting on, when he was called to the telephone. When he returned he said laconically, 'One of our boys has just bumped himself off.' When I asked what happened, he replied, 'Apparently he was just going out to the firing range, having reloaded and refuelled, when his motor stopped and he struck a house on landing.' The moment I heard this I had an awful feeling I knew the machine he was flying and asked if he knew the number of the machine. He told me and asked why. 'I flew that machine earlier this week and the engine cut with me, which I reported to the sergeant in charge.' When I spoke to the sergeant about the engine failure he was very upset. 'I went over the bloody thing with a toothcomb,' he said and called a fitter over to confirm how many ground-runs he had given the engine.

BOTH BARBARA AND I, before the war, had ample opportunities to mingle with what would now be called the 'jet-set'. We both agreed it was not the kind of life we wanted. I did not dislike meeting all the actors, actresses, politicians, royalty and heads of service and other VIPs who visited Castle Bromwich, but I was only really interested in a few individuals, and in the main it was a chore which interfered with the working programme, and for me a very tiring one as I had found out in the early days that ten minutes concentrated aerobatics was as taxing to my system as a whole day's normal test flying.

Incomparably the one person who excited me and I am sure the rest of the Castle Bromwich personnel more than anyone else was Mr Winston Churchill. Dick came over one afternoon and taking me to one side as we walked towards my office said, 'We've got the big man himself coming tomorrow, Alex, and they want to arrange a flying programme if you could organise for a demonstration—the Lord Mayor thought it would be a good idea if Mr Churchill could also see the Hurricane as well. Could you fix this up with Austin's?' As it was now my job to invite the pilot of the Austin Motor Company to bring over a Hurricane to Castle Bromwich and demonstrate it, I must confess to feeling a little uncomfortable. As host to a visitor I felt obliged to go out of my way to make sure the Austin pilot was made welcome, was kept in the limelight as much as the Spitfire and that there should be 'no scoring of points by the home-side'. This was more difficult to achieve than I realised at the time. The pilot was fairly well known to me and local people but needed introducing to all the press representatives. I was not helped in my task as the press badgered me with questions about the Spitfire rather like the favourite for the Derby on race day in the saddling enclosure.

During the flight briefing—to which I had given a great deal of careful consideration—I started to suggest that the Hurricane should demonstrate first but, remembering my manners, I checked myself in time and asked the Austin pilot which he would prefer. To my surprise he firmly asked to fly last and for each of us to demonstrate for seven minutes.

On the day two large black saloon cars arrived with Special Branch men in civilian clothes, I discussed security arrangements with them on the aerodrome and told them where to place their cars. Our Home Guard turned out, now complete with tin hats, rifles and fixed bayonets. The long black train of cars that made up the Prime Minister's party was enormous and as usual on an important occasion Mr and Mrs Churchill were introduced to selected people by Lord Dudley and they then chatted to the pilots and our Flight Shed personnel. I took off almost at once after the formalities were completed and went through my usual routine. This normally took six or seven minutes of tight, concentrated flying. It was unusual for me to be flying to the clock: at other times I would be completely and utterly absorbed in a short but very tense well-rehearsed programme. On this occasion I was anxious that the schedule should be adhered to exactly, so before my finale I thought it best to check with my wrist-watch. This was to be on what would have been my last dive to 400 IAS plus, at low level in front of the Prime Minister's party. At this point I would do a half-roll so that the Spitfire went by the audience inverted and I would then push the nose up firmly so that the machine would go into a steep vertical climb (without power as the engine would only 'windmill' inverted) and I would hold the climb until the machine had lost momentum but not all control and could be gently pulled over to complete the top of a loop followed by a dive and an aileron turn, pulling out again in front of the onlookers. I could, however, only get in the aileron turn if I had started the manoeuvre with a little height in hand.

This time I had started the inverted climb at below hangar height so that I knew I could not have room for the aileron turn but could just nicely get in a rather tight final dive to finish off with a half-roll, a chassis 'up' in the inverted position and a tight low high-'G' gliding turn to throw off excess speed for landing on the spot from which we had taken-off. It may sound rather silly but I reckoned the best time for me to look at my watch was after the half-roll from the high-speed dive, which required intense concentration at such low altitudes, and when I had pushed the nose up into the inverted climb and would have the customary wait for the momentum to be lost. This I very foolishly did. The break in my concentration was such that when the Spitfire nose was eased over so that I was pointing vertically at the ground I realised with a great shock that in looking at my watch I had lost those few vital feet at the end of the inverted climb and that I had left myself too small a margin in which to pull out.

Every type of machine varies in its response to the elevators under high 'G' loads. In the case of the Spitfire this also varied with different models but with the Mark V, provided a shock stall was not induced or the camera-door flap left unfastened, the degree of control was positive. When one is plummeting down to earth vertically, however, and the margin is extremely close there is an almost overwhelming desire to pull the machine harder and sooner than one should, and sometimes the result can be rather like roughly handling a very spirited blood horse with a soft mouth, but with more calamitous effect. In this particular instance there was no trouble and as I dived past and rolled over again and landed, no one would have known anything different from all the dozens of other shows I had given. But inwardly I knew that I must never allow my concentration to be broken again under such circumstances.

When I jumped down from the cockpit, I was surprised to be told by Lord Dudley that the Prime Minister wanted to see me again and with his ADC Commander Thompson as escort, I was taken through the small crowd to where the Prime

Minister stood. I did not know who gave the orders for I certainly did not hear any instructions, but in minutes chairs had been brought from my own office nearby by security men and I found myself being pushed into a chair next to the Prime Minister, a little later to be joined by Mrs Churchill. Again I saw no movement or instructions given, but Commander Thompson was obviously aware of the Prime Minister's wishes as I found I was virtually alone with Mr and Mrs Churchill and surrounding us at a discreet distance were other members of the party, including sharp-eyed security men. In the passing of time it is difficult to remember all our conversation. I do remember that the Prime Minister spoke about his early days of flying which I think he said started in 1912, the year I was born. He asked numerous questions and Mrs Churchill joined occasionally. We were interrupted as Lord Dudley sidled up with the Austin pilot to say the Prime Minister's train was waiting and that he was already well behind schedule. Most of the Marlborough family were there and as they came up to say good-bye the Duchess said with a laugh, 'My God, you put the wind up me.'

The Ministry officials and press were all delighted. It really was a beautiful day and the Castle Bromwich contingent looked like cats who had stolen the cream as everyone trooped by the Hurricane and Spitfire as they stood on the Flight Shed apron. Sometime later I had dinner with Lord Dudley at an American function. He came up to me and said, 'Did you hear from the Prime Minister?' I said, 'Yes, he very kindly sent me an autographed photograph of us taken on the airfield.' 'Well, you evidently made a great impression on him,' he went on. 'Do you know they had to keep the special train we had laid on waiting twenty minutes and we were supposed to be on a tight schedule.'

My father had always been a pro-Churchill man, so it was natural that I should also support him. Even before the war, I had followed his history and for me he symbolised at the most crucial stage in our fight for survival, what the true British nation was and all it stood for. I would always quarrel with anyone who said he was the greatest Englishman of the time. I always felt he was the greatest Englishman of *all* time: never before in the history of our people had one man alone saved the entire world. When I read today of how some politicians were prepared to negotiate a peace with Germany and in their own words, 'Churchill should not be permitted to stand in the way', I recapture the feelings and instincts prevalent at the time: that no other Englishman could have sustained us over such a long and bitter period with the faith that we would come through victorious. To me, meeting as I did so many Cabinet Ministers, chiefs of the Navy, Army and Air Force as well as heads of industry in America and in the Empire I felt quite apart from Churchill's superb oratory and control of the English language, his probing into every field of operations, it was his sheer personality that spoke for every one of us.

When George Snarey was posted from me and went back to Jeffrey Quill, I had to have another firm's pilot as replacement. The only available one at that time was Wing Commander Lowdell, who had recently joined the firm. When Dick asked me about him, I spoke the truth as I felt it: 'I've known George nearly all my flying life,' I said. 'He's a first-class pilot and in his younger days could have held his own with the best in the country. The only thing I worry about is his age, because he must be nearly forty and it is no joke shooting up and down to 20,000 ft or more a dozen times a day.' I need have had no fears, however. George, who had actually been a boy-entrant in the Royal Flying Corps, did his job well; he was not a technician but he had enough experience and commonsense to cope with most situations. He used to make me laugh in bad weather, though. George was of the old school and not very experienced in blind-flying. He was determined to pull his weight, however, and the first time we had thick, heavy cloud, he came down and said, 'I had to climb to over 20,000 ft before I reached the top.' I asked, 'What did you want to do that for? You could have checked the boost at 12,000 ft.' 'Oh yes, I know that,' he replied, 'but I couldn't turn until I got out of cloud. I'm all right on the straight and level, but I like to do my turns in the clear.'

With new pilots coming along fairly frequently I had to keep a systematic check on the standard of their work, and in the end I told Eric Holden and Jim Hastings to pick out one machine from each pilot for a monthly test check. This worked out quite well. I would OK the machine if it was all right and the pilot would have a report, which gave him confidence. In the early days the system had been somewhat loose, a hangover really from peacetime when every test pilot would have already proved himself before he was given the job. The result of this was that pilots had a fairly free hand and the chief pilot did not usually interfere unless absolutely necessary. I clamped down, however, when Hastings once came to me and said, 'Mr Henshaw, Flight Lieutenant —— has been flying a machine for three days now: he has had six aileron trims, he has had boost adjustment, and he has had revs altered and now he wants to have the wing changed, because it's flying left wing low.' I spoke to the pilot and then flew the machine; it certainly did not need a wing change.

On another occasion a very experienced pilot asked for an engine change but only told me in passing what he had done. Apparently the power was down about 1½ lb at rated altitude and I said it was most unusual for a new engine to be down on power as they are calibrated thoroughly before leaving the factory. 'Have you checked everything else out?' He said he had, and as the machine was already being returned to the factory I let it pass. I was away for the following two days and when I returned I wondered about this machine and asked for the test card. When I looked at it there were several crossings out and a figure of 8½ put in where it should have been 9 but with the ambient temperature given on the day of the test this would have brought it just within tolerance. I spoke to the pilot and said, 'This machine that you have had an engine change on, what was the result?' He coloured up and said, 'Well, it was all right, but only just.' I then asked, 'Did you check the boost gauge? Was there a leak? And did you calibrate the rev counter?' He answered that they changed the boost gauge; that there were no leaks; he had not thought about changing the rev counter. The machine was then on the delivery line but I told Eric Holden to inform AID that I wanted a retest. When I flew it, the aircraft was down nearly 2 lb at rated altitude and on landing there were some short, sharp words. Hastings took the rev counter out and it was found to be over 150 revs out at 3000 rpm.

At Castle Bromwich there was so much flying going on all day that it did not take me long to quickly assess the calibre of most of the pilots soon after they had arrived. One of the nicest men we had was an American, Ossy Snell, a really charming personality who came from Minneapolis. He and his brother had gone into Canada on the outbreak of war to join the RAF. They then transferred to the USAAF when the States came in after Pearl Harbor. Ossy so dearly wanted to join Vickers-Armstrongs that he persuaded me to visit his General and to ask him if he would post Ossy for test flying. Ossy had great difficulty in coping with our weather as well as the lack of radio and compass. It was rare for him to come back from a flight without me first having sent out an overdue signal, and when he did return he had found weather I never thought existed in the British Isles. He was popular with everyone, particularly as he would bring the other pilots more sugar and tinned fruit than they had seen since the outbreak of war.

At Cosford, as well as our own assembly plant, there was an RAF Maintenance Unit and from time to time I had seen a pilot flying one of their Spitfires with dash and elan. One afternoon I was completing a full-throttle climb when I became aware of another Spitfire creeping in alongside me. I had had a heavy day and was not in the mood for frolics, so I curtly acknowledged the pilot and went on taking my figures down. He came in so close that there would not have been room to have pushed in a matchbox. I knew he was trying to scare me, but I deliberately concentrated on my work, giving him occasionally a very bored look, but inwardly I thought: If that silly twit marks my machine I'll mark him when I get down. I finished the climb, came down to 10,000 ft to do a full-throttle level run and afterwards as I was about to dive for Cosford I saw the other Spitfire making for my tail. It was very often customary for two Spitfires, when meeting, to have a dog-fight and the winner was the one who could stay on the other's tail the longest. I had done this dozens of times and as a rule in two or three quick movements I was on the tail and there I would stay. I did this, but to my surprise the other Spitfire was still close as I looked in my rear mirror. I did it again with the same result. I was short of time and rattled that I had not thrown him off right away, so I decided to teach him a quick lesson. I pulled my machine into a full power vertical climb, watching the mirror as my opponent followed closely and then as the climb remained vertical but the speed fell away to below the stall, I snapped the throttle closed, held the controls rigidly and my Spitfire slid backwards on its tail stopping the propeller with the backward thrust and then snapped over, plummeting towards the ground. We were already quite low when I had done this and as I dived with the prop still stationary, I made for a belt of high trees. I shot round these just as the prop turned and the engine burst into life, and looked up to where I expected the other Spitfire to be, so that I could take him, but he was nowhere in sight. The pilot, as I found out later, was a Czech, Venda Jicha, and he told me that he was so surprised at what had happened and scared he might have caused an accident as I went down, that he cleared off for home.

After the first occasion of our meeting in the air, I did not make contact with him for another week or so, and this time I had time to spare and was more than willing to test his mettle. This time I pulled out every trick in the bag and having got on his tail twice and stayed there I was about to wave 'Cheerio' when I noticed a panel in the fuselage near the tail of his aircraft flexing as he operated the elevators. Closing up I signalled that something was wrong and beckoned him to follow me to Castle Bromwich. We put a stiffener in the panel and I had the opportunity to speak with him. When he left me he said, 'If only I could get a job like yours.' 'If you would like to apply for a posting,' I answered, 'I'll approve it when it comes through to me.' Within ten days he was at Castle Bromwich.

Venda Jicha was the best Spitfire pilot I ever had at Castle Bromwich. He had been in the Czechoslovakian Air Force and was then their top aerobatic pilot. He was a well-built boy, dark hair, Slavonic features, blue eyes, a firm mouth and a strong jaw. He looked a fighter and was a fighter: I would rather have had him on my side than against me. When the Germans moved into Sudetenland he watched them with the rest of his air force colleagues and then as they could do nothing with their machines under armed guard, he left his own country and asked to join the French air force. They would not accept him because France was not at war with Germany and persuaded Jicha to join the Foreign Legion. He served there under dreadful conditions until France declared war and then returned to join a French fighter squadron. He said the first time he went into action he led a flight with a Frenchman on either side in formation, they saw a squadron of Me 109s and as he went to engage he saw the two Frenchmen turn and leave him to face the Germans alone. With the fall of France he escaped and was posted to a Czech fighter squadron in England. It was a long time before I knew and understood him, but before he left me I think if I had said to him I was going to fly into Hell itself he would have followed me.

1942 began an ominously significant year for me. I had several straightforward forced landings, if you can call a dead-stick landing straightforward; these were mostly through oil pressure failures and one a seizure due to an internal glycol leak. On 3 January however, I had been in some physical pain all day and in the end had to pack up flying and get a works car to drive me home. Barbara rang the doctor and he recommended a dose of castor oil. When this did not ease the pain she rang him up again and he told her that the dose she had given me was too small. When I had taken the second dose I became so ill that Barbara insisted the doctor came out immediately. On arrival he took one look and rushed to the telephone to call an ambulance, get me a bed in hospital and ask a surgeon if he could operate within the hour. The resulting operation put me off flying for three months, which I spent dealing with my own affairs and buying farms and real estate in Barbara's name, so that if the worst happened to me and we won the war, at least she would be secure.

Towards the end of my three months recuperation period I helped Dick with the continuous round of factory visitors and kept an eye on the flying side at the same time. Wing Commander Lowdell took over when I was ill and we had on duty at that time Captain Snell, Flight Lieutenant Ulstad, Flight Lieutenant Rosser, Flight Lieutenant Jicha, Flight Lieutenant Huntley, Flight Lieutenant Lamb, Flight Lieutenant Lowe and Flight Lieutenant Johnson. The first thing that greeted me on my return was a report from Lowdell about Jicha. 'You'll have to post him, Alex,' said George. I said, 'Why? He seems a good pilot to me.' 'Oh yes, he's very good indeed,' George replied. 'But there is a nasty atmosphere developing and if it had not been for the fact that I knew you would be coming back, I would have had him posted.' I was disappointed and said that now I was able to fly again I would have a word with Jicha.

Olaf Ulstad, the Norwegian pilot, was a shrewd, intelligent man; not the most experienced of our pilots he had trained as a barrister and was good company with whom to talk. We always got on together extremely well. He was also something of a Don Juan and always had a string of girl friends in tow. There was nothing sissy about Olaf, however, and as a boxer of some repute his idea of a good evening was to visit London, drink some of the lethal spirits that were being sold as whisky during the war, and if he got into a real brawl, particularly with American sailors, this rounded off a good night's entertainment. He fought for the Finns against the Russians, and his stories of that campaign made Hammond Innes' books seem like children's fairy stories. In one engagement the Finns knew a Russian attack in strength was imminent, and they had strengthened their positions with concrete emplacements, heavily supported by numerous machine-gun batteries. When the attack started Olaf said it could not possibly succeed as it was made by infantry across an open plain without artillery or tank support. The Russians were mown down in their thousands, but when the attack should have stopped because of the hopelessness of the situation the infantry still advanced from their grouping positions in distant trenches. The climax came when, although the Russians were slowed down considerably as wave after wave had to climb over large mounds of bodies of their dead comrades, the Finns were running out of ammunition and those groups who did have plenty were in trouble with their guns running hot. Just when the position became critical and the order was given to fix bayonets, the attack stopped as suddenly as it had begun. When later a state of war existed between Germany and Russia, Olaf escaped into Russia and made his way to America via Murmansk and Odessa. On the way he did a very foolish thing, which very nearly cost him his life. He was engaged at one time to President Mannerheim's niece and with some influence travelled as a Norwegian diplomat with sealed briefcase. On entry into Russia he was asked to open the briefcase. For his service in Finland he had been awarded the Finnish Cross, and he had foolishly carried this with him in the sealed briefcase, knowing that if the military award for combat against the Russians were found he would be shot without trial. He had only one choice, to try and bluff it out; apparently he shouted and stormed to such effect that the Russians let him through without opening the case, but it was a very near thing.

'What's the trouble with Jicha, Olaf?' I asked. He was

silent for a moment and then said, 'Jicha is a Slav. He is also a very good pilot and he dislikes being told when not to fly. I think he feels we are a lot of softies.' I decided to wait and watch before I made the final decision to post Jicha. A few mornings later, before I had resumed active control, George was briefing the pilots; the weather was flyable, but certainly not good and he had told them to hold off a bit until it had improved. At that Jicha snorted and stormed out of the office. In a flash I had guessed what was going through Jicha's mind and said to George. 'There's your trouble George; he thinks he's the only one with any guts. I think he's got a lot to learn but doesn't know it yet.'

The normal practice in peacetime was for the Commanding Officer of flying to determine if the weather was suitable for all to fly and George had followed this practice, with which I would not disagree. I had realised early on at Castle Bromwich, however, that if I were to adopt this practice we should very often be so far behind with our flying programme that it would be serious not only from the testing point of view but the Flight Shed itself would not be able to cope; there would be severe build-up in delivery delays, to say nothing of the problems related to the maintenance units and the squadrons. With each pilot, when he was posted to me, I would spend considerable time: detailing what was required on his test reports; allocating his flight test area, a V-shaped sector of about 15–20° radiating from base, in which he could climb in cloud without fear of colliding with our other machines, also on test. I would also discuss the danger points such as high ground in low cloud, and balloon cables. There was also the unusually sinister hazard of the Hams Hall cooling towers, constantly belching out steam which in bad conditions mingled with the murk and low cloud; if one was unwary it was quite possible to make a careful descent right into the mouths of these huge towers with of course disastrous results. Finally I would say, 'Never think you have to fly in bad weather because I do. I have had more experience than you. I know the area better and I know where the hazards are. There is a war on and it is up to everyone to do their best, but on no account take unnecessary risks. Bear this in mind: every pilot and aircraft we lose on this job is one up to the enemy.' The result of this was that we kept pace with the demands. Sometimes there was certainly a day's backlog in conditions of thick fog, but in the main the system worked well. I got to know a great many local tricks as there were times, under severe pressure, when I would fly twenty machines a day and would be the only one to leave the ground. Strangely there were, as far as I know, no hard or bitter feelings anywhere, and as I said to the other pilots, I had been there so long that Hams Hall printed a message in the sky for me every day. This was to some extent true, as in very low cloud and bad visibility I got to know what would happen to the steam from my friends the towers. In low stratus it just belched in a long plume way above, which could be seen for miles. In other conditions it was less discernible, but to the practised eye it could be picked out and with long experience I was agreeably surprised at the accuracy with which I could break cloud in bad conditions with my nose almost on the aerodrome boundary.

I kept off Spitfires for a while until my stomach muscles built up from the operation, and flew only Wellingtons and the communications aircraft. Jicha came in again one morning in dubious conditions and said in a sarcastic voice to all in general, 'No flying today, of course.' George Lowdell looked at me and nothing was said, but I had made up my mind to teach Jicha a lesson when the opportunity arose, before I had him posted.

The occasion came some weeks later. I was feeling fit and on form but had driven in by car instead of on my bicycle as the weather was so foul. It was blowing a full gale with very heavy rain squalls and the morning was dark with heavy cloud sweeping across the sky 300–400 ft from the ground. I hadn't thought of flying until it struck me that this was the opportunity for which I had been waiting. As Hastings greeted me from the car with a grin saying, 'Hardly cycling weather, is it, sir?' I replied, 'No, you're dead right Jim; but get two Spitfires ready will you.' I put on my flying suit and as Jicha came into the office I said, 'Well, Venda, what's holding you up this morning? We have got at least thirty machines to clear up.' He thought I was joking and grimaced and sat down. At that moment Eric Holden tapped on the door and said, 'The first machine's ready for test.' I said, 'Venda, will you take it or shall I?' He looked out of the windows battered by the rain and coloured up. 'No one's going to fly in this,' he said.

I ran through the deluge quickly to the waiting Spitfire and slammed the hood closed whilst I strapped on the parachute and Sutton harness with the rain beating a noisy tattoo on the wings. I knew I had to be careful, otherwise with the wind gusting as it was I wouldn't even get off the ground. Fortunately the wind was from the south-west, the direction the machine was already pointed on the run-up base, and I was airborne almost as I opened the throttle. At 17,000 ft I broke through the top of the cloud into blinding sunlight and I did one steep dive allowing for the wind and broke base just about where I expected to with a nice margin to spare.

When I landed I saw the men were struggling in heavy oilskins to get the other Spitfire ready. As the office door slammed behind me and I wiped the rain from my face, George asked, 'Is it as grim as it looks?' I looked hard at Venda and said, 'No, it's not bad at all, just the weather Jicha's been waiting for.' Jicha, who had his flying gear on said, 'How thick does it go up?' When I told him he said he would take the next machine. I said, 'Hold on, I'll go with you.' What I really meant was, you're not going to get away with a quick low circuit if I can help it.

Both machines were on the apron side by side with men hanging on to each wing. When we were both ready I gave a thumbs-up sign to Venda and we took off together. Before we entered cloud I tucked in tight on his starboard side and as he grimaced to me I pointed upwards. We had plenty of time to look at one another as we bucked our way through the cloud

and I think we could both re...
As we broke into the sunshine a...
to fall back and come in alongsi...
formation flying and I signalled to...
position ourselves for the dive down,...
leech and we bucked and hurtled our w...
tearing over the screen and beating at the...
As we slowed down and broke cloud I signa...
away and we both landed within seconds ...ther.
Nothing was said as we struggled against wind a... in to the
office, but the change could be sensed by everyone. From then
on Jicha was a different person.

IT WAS INEVITABLE that with the constant nightly bombing, materials and equipment were always in short supply, manpower and communications and transport continually disrupted and of course the normal constant flow of production virtually impossible to maintain. This meant that other problems of a different nature were created in our Flight Sheds. The odd thing in the administration of this department was that although I was officially only in charge of the pilots and our flying programmes at Castle Bromwich and elsewhere, in spite of having the Liaison Manager Kingsley Wood, it seemed that the management looked to me for any decision of importance connected with the aerodrome side of the factory. For my part I was constantly searching my mind for new and better systems to improve our working efficiency. I was aware more than most that we had a large wastage of manpower in the Flight Shed. Pilots were on the go at all times, unless prevented by weather, as there was always a job to do, if not at Castle Bromwich then at one of the other units; but the one thing that caused me more headaches than anything else was the fact that I would meet the chargehands with Hastings in the morning and dozens of men would be hanging around for work until some of the machines arrived from the factory and tests began. Often nothing would arrive until late in the afternoon and then we would have to deal with twenty or thirty machines all at once, which meant night shifts and flying at first light. As we could not afford to lay men off, I thought of a scheme to put the men on to a piece-work job producing Spitfire parts such as ailerons or wingtips when there was no work to do on production machines. I discussed this idea with Dick and he agreed in principle that the idea was good; he then asked Reg Leech, the Production Manager, to examine the scheme in detail and evaluate it. Reg discussed it with me and it was soon apparent there were other side issues which would make the plan, if not unworkable, certainly uneconomic.

I was not only worried about the loss in manpower but I had to consider the psychological aspect. With a good team it is necessary to have every man pulling his weight if one is to get good results and it hurt me to see these men standing around talking and wasting time through no fault of their own, whilst others were continually overworked. Having had my first scheme rejected my mind turned to something else. In the early days I could either go over to the senior mess at the factory, eat at the RAF mess on the aerodrome or have our food sent over by the canteen. I would have settled for the canteen food, which was not very good, but when Dick heard about this he insisted that a proper kitchen be installed for my personal use and that of the other pilots and visitors. This was a luxury appreciated by us all and we had good food most of the time and a first-class cook available from 8 in the morning until 5 in the afternoon. I was shocked, however, by the wastage that went on, with apparent disregard for the critical situation worsening daily as the U-boat pack found our convoys; Barbara, like other ordinary people, found great difficulty in putting on a square meal each day. I thought the answer in so far as our own circumstances were concerned was a pig club. I discussed this with Dick and he thought the idea was good, but I think fearing the extent of my enthusiasm, refrained from taking any part in it. I then rang up the catering manager and when he told me the canteen waste and swill was collected and no payment made, I said we would take it over on the same terms. He was somewhat shaken but dare not refuse. I then got a dozen or so of the men I knew and could trust, and between us we thrashed out a scheme to get our plans moving. At the back of the enormous Flight Shed blocks there was a large pile of railway sleepers, stacked up against the old railway embankment. They had not been used for years so, as they were on MAP property, I decided without more ado to 'borrow' them. I should think amongst our men we had almost every type of tradesman imaginable and in no time at all when there was nothing to do in the Flight Shed, I would put them to work building the pigsties. They worked with such enthusiasm that within the month we had not only a long range of very suitable buildings, but some of the ex-farmer employees had brought in sows and boars so that the rear of the Flight Shed began to smell and sound rather like a substantial pig farm. The wastage in swill from the factories sometimes made me seethe: it was nothing to have several large sacks of good bread loaves, a score or more of perfectly fresh ox-tails or other edible meat mixed in with enormous quantities of really good quality food, all of which we boiled and mixed up with our rationed quota of pig meal. In a very short while we had so many pigs that a decision had to be made as to where to put them. I was tempted to wire off part of the aerodrome but as there were other problems involved, decided against it. I then called in one of our electricians and asked him to make up an electric fence, which we strung around all the usable land at the rear of the Flight Sheds and adjoining the sties. This was almost the perfect answer until at odd times the wire broke and then there was pandemonium as pigs were chasing and squealing and grunting all over the place. The Castle Bromwich Pig Club was instantly an enormous success: not only did every member have pork regularly and bacon frequently but when we wound up at the end of the war everyone had a substantial block of Government Savings Bonds to his credit.

At times I had opposition from certain quarters and one small attack was quite unexpected. I always made a point that any man could see me personally if he was not satisfied and when Hastings said there was an employee representing the RSPCA who would like to speak to me about the pigs, I told him to send him over in his tea-break. The man was quite sincere and his complaint was that the electrified wire was cruel to the pigs. Now unknown to him I had spent a long time working out a shock voltage which would keep the pigs away from the wire without hurting them, and with the electrician I had tested this carefully with wet feet and hands to get it right. However, I kept a straight face during the discussion and said seriously, 'You know if I were a pig and I put my wet nose against a piece of wire and it gave me a shock, I don't think I would do it twice; and if I did I'd deserve all I got.' The man paused and then said, 'You know sir, I never thought of it that way. Of course it's up to the pig.'

Discipline among the pilots was nearly always good; in fact with a few exceptions a very friendly comrade-like spirit prevailed. Jicha now fitted in like the rest, except he was much closer to me; and I could rely on him for almost anything as he was far and away the best pilot I had. Sometimes there were petty grievances; before Jicha got to know me well he would come to me with some tale of Olaf's exploits and expect me to take some action. I would say, 'Look Venda, I'm not concerned with the pilots' private affairs; as long as they do their job properly, they can do what the hell they like provided I don't see them do it. In any case how do you know what you are telling me is true?' And Venda would then shock me and in true Bohemian-Slavonic style tell me how he had read Olaf's letters. I started to tell him that he couldn't do that sort of thing and then when I saw it was a waste of time, I burst out laughing at the ludicrousness of the situation. This made Venda angry and he did not bring the subject up again.

In the early years, as our pilots were nearly always picked men, they were in the main not only competent, but well-mannered and behaved; as the years passed by it was to be expected that the standard would drop somewhat, but I am pleased to recollect that out of all the numerous pilots that passed through my hands only about two had to be posted or dealt with, and in general they were excellent pilots, good men and in many instances friends whom I was proud to have. At first I liked to have all the pilots in my own office, which was quite large, as I could then talk shop to them and this helped the work along. I was, however, shaken one day when I received a confidential report on the misuse of my priority telephone. Attached to this report was a verbatim copy of the conversation of one of the Flight Lieutenants talking to his girl friend 300 miles away, in a language that I am quite sure Miss Cook, my secretary, had not overheard. To make matters worse, Anderson the Commercial Manager had rung me up to say he had instructed the priority telephone to be taken out and I had jumped down his throat to such an extent that he said he was going to see the Managing Director immediately. When Dick saw me about it we both saw the funny side but at the same time realised the seriousness. I dealt with the pilot concerned and then ruled that only two senior pilots would share my office and the others would go into other suitable premises. I was sorry for Miss Cook as she was a first-class secretary and had been with me since the early days of the war and had shared my office; but I felt she must also have an office of her own with so much work in hand.

If we had the odd man out I soon knew of it because of Venda's temperament. One pilot we had just did not fit in, but as I was sorry for him I let the matter slide until one day I saw Venda seething. When I asked what was troubling him he told me the details and then said, 'I'm going to take him out on the airfield and beat him up.' I replied sharply, 'You'll do no such thing. I'll look into this and if what you say is true, he'll go.' Unfortunately the story was true and I suspended the pilot immediately and neither Venda nor the pilot concerned saw each other again. Other incidents occurred at times. One rather flamboyant character of good education and family kept a large sports car, had plenty to say for himself, but was only a very moderate pilot. One day Hastings came in and said, 'I don't like doing this, sir, but I feel you ought to know that the Flight Lieutenant has asked O'Rourke to fill his car up with oil. O'Rourke did as he was told of course, but reported it to me.' I said to Hastings, 'Say nothing about this to anyone, but tell O'Rourke he did the right thing.' I called the pilot concerned into the office, and he asked quite blandly, what was a gallon or so of oil when we used thousands daily? I said, 'I'm not concerned with your trivial requirements; I'm more anxious about the effect this will have on the men, if they know the pilots are getting away with what is to put it bluntly, petty pilfering.' Although I knew at the time there was no such intention it was undoubtedly how the fitters had interpreted it and he would never live it down at Castle Bromwich. I followed on, 'I'm not going to make out a report on this incident and no one will hear about it from me, but you are to go over to Wing Commander Becker, the Overseer, and tell him you want a posting at once. You may use what excuse you like, but provided you go nothing will be said. If you don't, then I have no alternative but to file a report on the matter.' Becker rang me up that afternoon and said that the Flight Lieutenant had applied for a transfer and what was he to do? I suggested that he dealt with the matter right away, and I would fill in his conduct report, which would be a satisfactory one.

Some of the service pilots were permanently commissioned but in the main they were either volunteers or conscripted. A few had transferred from other services, such as Flight Lieutenant Huntley. He was a quiet, gentlemanly type, whom I liked at once. He had held a higher rank in the army and I asked him, 'Why did you transfer to the RAF, Geoffrey?' He said, 'Well, frankly I thought I would find the RAF life easier. I liked the army life but I was in charge of a field battery: when we had to do forced night movements in the pouring rain and then at dawn when we were all frozen, I had to plot a creeping barrage over the heads of our own infantry I began to think there must be an easier way of fighting a war.'

Once I had some RAF Maintenance Unit test pilots attached to me for a few hours. Becker came over to my office and said, 'Alex, it has been suggested that it might be a good idea if some of the maintenance unit pilots were to be sent to you. They could observe at first hand the test flight procedures and they could assist in the general programme, and anywhere else you cared to send them.' I replied that it would be a good idea, but they would have to be a part of the test group and subject to the same briefing instructions.

This arrangement did not last long and it proved to be not a very good idea. As I reflect back over the years I think unintentionally we expected too much and were a little unkind to the MU pilots. To start with, although most of my team were young serving officers with rather low hours, they had been selected for the posting so it was assumed they had the aptitude for the job and all had combat experience with the Spitfire. I also spent a great deal of time with most of them either briefing or talking shop and of course their work would be carefully checked before they were put on their own. During this period of time they also became familiar with the local terrain and quickly devised their own methods of finding their way about.

MU pilots who were sent to us were really thrown in at the deep end. They varied in age and experience considerably— they may not have done many hours in a Spitfire and one said that he had not been over 7000 ft for years! They were not helped by the enormous industrial area either, as it was certainly not the district I would choose for testing fighters in wintertime. Finally none were happy flying blind without radio or navigational aids and the numerous balloon cables all around only added to their problems.

Whilst the work was routine for our own pilots, they had been trained to work on a set procedure and knew what to look for and also what to expect. Routine procedure was essential, not only for the pilots but also for our groundstaff: it is no use spending hours on a fine boost adjustment during the initial flights at low altitude if later on you find that at 15–20,000 ft you have a boost-line leak, a wrongly calibrated rev-counter or even a faulty boost-gauge. Neither is it any use calling for maximum elevator trim-tab adjustment because of lack of control in the dive when the trouble lies in the tailplane.

The RAF became aware of some weakness in their own

training and founded the Empire Test Pilots' School at Boscombe Down, in 1943, which no doubt went a long way to alleviating many obvious shortcomings. I never went to the school, nor did I ever really consider that I was a test pilot. True I was doing it as a war job and there were many aspects with which I felt happy and at home but certainly in peacetime I would not from choice have picked it as a career. Nor did I have a degree in engineering or aeronautics.

Many assume that a test pilot must also be an outstanding airman. I do not feel that this necessarily need be so, although most of the test pilots I knew were. Certainly one must know what is going on both in the engine and with the airframe and mentally must analyse the behaviour of both. I think one of the greatest assets is not only to have this ability but at the same time to be able to impart the knowledge, the analysis and the assessment in an articulate manner to the technical and groundstaff responsible for putting any ideas the pilot may have expounded into operation.

My own experience and training was self-taught in the pre-war period preparing aircraft for racing and record-breaking. I quickly learned that the first thing to do was to get my priorities right and in balance.

More MU pilots arrived, but at the same time the weather retained its usual dreary, cold, depressing winter cloak. They mingled well with our own pilots, some of whom were coping with the uncomfortable conditions and who explained to the others on landing the essential points for getting in the tests and also how to find your way back to base. The scheme terminated abruptly, however, when the officer in charge of the pilots said he had received a telephone call from his own base to return as soon as possible.

Becker came over shortly afterwards full of enthusiasm to say how successful the idea had been. The MU pilots had, for the first time, been shown certain aspects and an extensive programme of work they had not before appreciated. The exchange had done a tremendous amount of good all round.

On reflection I think the idea may have originated as a result of a particular Spitfire which had done the rounds of the MUs in an effort to cure severe and critical vibration at high speeds, and which in the end was sent to us from Little Rissington for a report and suggested change of wings. The report that we sent back must have been so unbelievable that it gave rise to suspicious and caustic remarks. When the machine was first delivered and I saw the long report, I asked Flight Lieutenant Rosser to do a check flight; he soon came down confirming what had previously been reported, with the remark, 'I don't know what the hell it is, but it scared me to death.' When I told Jicha who had stood by laughing to do a test run he also landed soon afterwards and in his broken English confirmed Rosser's report with a more descriptive viewpoint; at first he could find nothing wrong, but as the speed increased in the dive the machine suddenly started to shake and vibrate to such an extent that he thought it would break up in the air. He prepared to jump for it, but as he did so the vibration ceased completely and he had landed, thankful to get down. I then took off, puzzled and very much on my mettle as both Rosser and Jicha had reported the machine being perfectly normal, other than when this vibration set in. Every dial and gauge read correctly, the controls were average as was the performance; I did a series of mild aerobatics and the aircraft still appeared OK to me, so that I was more puzzled than ever as I strained to hear the slightest tremor or unusual sound. I stepped up the aerobatics and then, as I dived for some vertical rolls, like an explosion the machine suddenly shook and vibrated, so that like Jicha I hastily prepared to bail out; but as suddenly as it started the staccato noise and vibration stopped. I flew around for a while mulling the matter over in my mind and then to find out more I decided I would do a series of dives at high altitude and take down some figures.

At about 430 IAS in the first dive the vibration set in again and I had to brace myself to set down the figures I wanted; as

I did so it came to me that I could read all the gauges quite clearly and that again they were all normal and I decided to continue the dive but be ready for any breakup, as far as I was able. I have always been conscious of the manner in which mind and imagination control to a great extent one's physical reactions, and I began to realise that we had all been hoodwinked: we were getting vibration on this machine, yes, but most of it was a rapid-frequency staccato sound, which whilst disturbing to the mind appeared unharmful to the machine. I then momentarily took my hands off the controls as we dived and pressed them both over my ears, so that the noise was almost fully damped out: to my pleasant surprise the machine behaved like any other Spitfire at that speed. I now felt I had the key to the problem, but where was the noise originating? Pulling out of the dive I climbed up again and set the machine into a fast, prolonged dive, this time mentally prepared for the vibration and noise when it started; I felt all round the cockpit and thought I could feel a hard persistent hammering near the engine. I was sure it had nothing to do with the engine or airscrew, but it appeared to be coming mostly from the engine bulkhead or even the main petrol tank. Then suddenly it came to me with such simplicity and suddenness that I couldn't resist shouting to myself for being such a bloody fool as not to guess the reason on the first flight. The top petrol tank was covered with a thick, hard covering of self-sealer beneath the heavy bullet-proof armour plating. I was sure that this self-sealer was split and had become detached, so that when the speed built up in a dive this flapped so vigorously between the armour plating and an almost empty petrol tank that the noise was like a kettle-drummer gone mad. I was going to have some fun with Rosser and Jicha when I landed. They were waiting for the touchdown and I said to Jicha, 'I'm surprised at you, Venda; an experienced test pilot and you nearly threw a perfectly good aircraft away, because you're scared of a piece of rubber flapping.' When I told them what I thought had happened, neither of them would believe me, but sure enough, when later they had the tank out, it was obvious what had taken place. Whilst I was pleased we had traced the trouble, I was angry when I totted up the hours of test flying the machine had done, complete with engine and prop change before the maintenance units had decided to return it to us.

About that time I was finding it difficult to cope with the Cowley Spitfires, as my own commitments were increasing considerably, so that when I saw Sir Miles Thomas at Oxford and he suggested that they obtain their own resident pilot, I was more than ready to concur with the arrangement, and promised to brief their pilot when they had engaged him. I had some pleasant times at Cowley and had many friends amongst the former car-building industry.

After Dick Reynell was killed, John Grierson was appointed in his place, and occasionally when time permitted we would run out to a quiet Oxfordshire pub and have a meal together. I had known John Grierson for some time. A quiet, serious, modest Scot, he was well known in peacetime by his personal insignia of *rouge et noir*: he had his Gipsy Moth painted in red and black, but not as one would expect; he had split the machine precisely down the middle so that when one viewed it from the port side it would be an apparently all-black machine, and then as one walked round to the starboard side it would appear to be all in red. He had treated his car in precisely the same manner. Whilst not necessarily accepting it as a suitable decor, one had to admit it had its amusing side as one watched strangers stop in their tracks and with un-believing eyes walk back for a second look. This flamboyancy was I felt quite out of keeping with John's normal quiet character and I meant many times to ask him why he had done it but never got round to it.

As was understandable there was little or no publicity given to our work during the war years; nevertheless I found I was being called upon with increasing regularity to demonstrate the Spitfire at various RAF stations all over the country, and wherever possible I would try to fit it in. Many would be for a special occasion such as a parade or sports day event and I'm afraid I caused minor grievances on numerous occasions as, although I would try my best to give a show at the exact time arranged, more often than not I would not land but return to Castle Bromwich, South Marston, Cosford, Desford or wherever I had taken the machine from. My point of view was that if I stayed for a meal or tea I had to be presentable myself and change, which was not easy when flying all day; and also it meant the machine being out of action for longer than need be.

Writers and reporters came at times for personal interviews by arrangement with the Ministry of Aircraft Production and I know Dick, as the Managing Director, was more than pleased that they should do so; but at times this caused jealousy and caustic remarks from other quarters. Godfrey Winn asked to interview me in my office at Castle Bromwich once and wrote a whole page in the *Sunday Express* which, to say the least, was somewhat flattering, being headed in large letters, 'Spitfire Wizard'. The first result was a sarcastic note from Supermarines to Dick which he showed to me laughing at such small-mindedness.

Once Dick asked me to take a Spitfire over to a neighbouring aerodrome, Baginton, where an important American visitor was examining the Armstrong Whitworth Whitley and as he had not the time to come on to Castle Bromwich I was to arrange with the Armstrong Whitworth chief test pilot to demonstrate the Spitfire there. After an amicable discussion on the merits of the fighter with the American I took off and conscious once again that I was flying to a critical audience in having the chief test pilot of a rival firm to watch, I flew as accurately and as well as I was able. Months later I saw Jeffrey at Hursley Park during a conference and laughingly he said, 'You shook them at Coventry when you were over there. They said it was quite suicidal. The chief test pilot gave you less than three months at the most as no one could fly like that and live for long.'

Miss Cook had left a note on my desk when I returned:

'Would Mr Alex Henshaw have lunch with the Duke of Marlborough and if so kindly confirm?' I flew over as arranged and the Duke with Lady Sarah Churchill was waiting for me on the aerodrome with an enormous Rolls. I guessed the Duke would have asked other members of the family to lunch to see the Spitfire perform so, to save any awkwardness, I said, 'Did you want anyone in particular to see the machine, sir?' He replied, 'We would *all* like to come back after lunch and see you fly, if that can be arranged.' I asked the officer in charge of the control tower to put me through to the Commanding Officer, and not saying who was there asked if I might give a demonstration with the Spitfire that afternoon. To my surprise I was told curtly that this was a bomber training centre and although it was Sunday afternoon with no flying, the Commanding Officer did not wish to encourage or condone such lightheartedness and would prefer if I did not buzz his aerodrome. I said nothing to the CO but, turning to the Duke, I said, 'The Commanding Officer does not view my flying with favour. Do you mind if I choose a quiet spot on our way to lunch where you can all watch in comfort, and it will be outside the Station Commander's jurisdiction?'

When we turned up the magnificent drive and stopped at the bottom of the enormous stone stairway, a manservant immediately came down and opened the door of the Rolls. In the drawing room, as large as the whole of a normal house, I was greeted by Lord and Lady Dudley and then introduced to all the other members present. I have forgotten what we had for lunch, but I know I enjoyed it, also the conversation which was by no means dull. After we had spent some time over our coffee, we all set off in a train of cars, which had appeared from nowhere. I paid my respects to all as I was leaving, when they stopped their cars in a beautiful open glade set in the magnificent wooded countryside nearby and I promised they would be able to see the Spitfire perform in a few minutes. The setting was ideal and having performed for ten or fifteen minutes I set course back for Castle Bromwich.

It is hard to remember the worst period of the war after so many years, but I think it must have been at about this time. Although hope sprang eternal, on quiet reflective analysis, it was very difficult, in fact almost impossible, to see how we were going to survive the grim struggle in which we seemed to be held relentlessly by the throat. The midland industrial area in such circumstances in the midst of a typical English winter was depressing in the extreme. We had of course no social life worthy of note. In our own home Barbara and I worked for peace of mind and also to alleviate a worsening food situation.

As I pushed my cycle out of the drive in the dull light of an early winter morning, the all-clear signal would go more often than not after a continuous night's bombing on Birmingham, Coventry, Leicester or Wolverhampton. The same would happen in the evening as I cycled home: the sirens would wail, the guns would blast off, the balloons shoot up and the searchlights probe the sky, making the whole picture so unreal that it was difficult to remind oneself of the life we used to live. By that time I was well known locally and often if I had an early morning job to do I would use the Tomtit and land next to the house. Sometimes, although I was only a few minutes away from the factory, I would cut this a little bit fine. I would probably try to get a final flight in before dusk, in a Spitfire, so that by the time I took off in the Tomtit it was almost dark with the balloons already up, the sirens wailing and the guns going off as if all hell was let loose. I did not have lights on the Tomtit but would follow the Coleshill main road by the dull glowworm signal of the odd car lights to the Meriden crossroads and then turn right until I picked out the dark shadows of the trees that surrounded my field. There was a gun battery nearby but they knew my aircraft and would pause to let me in before they blazed away into, as far as I could see, the black, empty sky. Before I got them educated it was a bit dicey as it is not funny to see red tracer catching up with you with the feeling that any second the thing is going to explode inside your petrol tank.

The first time this happened was in broad daylight, when the air raid alarm had just been given and I was flying low and fast in a Spitfire to get out of the area so that the test flying could carry on normally. I had just passed a battery I knew well when I was more than surprised to see tracer coming at me with alarming speed, so that I dived almost onto the ground and weaved in between any obstacle I could see. Later when I landed I rang up the Battery Commander and, as he sounded young and confused, I used some very earthy language for his benefit: 'If your bloody erks can't tell a Spitfire from a Junkers 88 then they ought not to be manning that pop-gun of yours. And in any case I've got enough trouble of my own without having the Army trying to fire tracer up my arse!' The young CO laughed and from then on we had wonderful co-operation between us.

My brother Leslie had now been sent out to the Far East from the earlier unhappy campaigns in the Western Desert and he wrote me a letter which upset and depressed me and, as it was uncensored, I wondered how it had got through. He wrote such was the confusion and chaos that as his convoy moved into Rangoon another convoy moved out. First they were told to destroy Rangoon and advance to India and then, when on the way, they were ordered with a special pep talk to return and hold Rangoon to the last. He went on to say that they were practically surrounded and were being strafed night and day by enemy aircraft without a single fighter to put into the sky against them. He thought that this would be the last I would hear from him, the letter ended. I was naturally upset and, when after the war was over, he told me the rest of the story I knew I had reason to be. They could not hold Rangoon long, so they tried to break through the Jap lines in their lorries and ambulances with the Japs sniping from the jungle as they moved along. They began to run out of ammunition and trucks broke down. The problem was not helped by the fact that they were ordered to destroy everything that would be of help to the enemy and proceed individually on foot in the direction of

India. Leslie said, 'The sight of sending hundreds of almost brand-new trucks and ambulances over into a ravine with their engines screaming flat out, with no oil in the sumps, was enough to make tough battle-hardened men weep.' The prisoners were treated in the desperate spirit of the time. My brother survived with a kukri and rifle, but it must have been one of the longest individual retreats in the history of the British Army.

Barbara had to go into hospital for a few days for an operation. It was not serious but I worried and tried to get to her as early as possible each day. The weather had been wet and poor for some time so that, although we were up to date with the test work, there was a heavy backlog on the collection of tested aircraft. Hastings had come to me and said he could not find enough room on the perimeter to disperse them. The east side of Castle Bromwich was at that time newly made up ground, re-seeded and unusable by heavy machines, so I told him to have them spaced out in that area. Before leaving the house I had fed Tony, the ducks and chickens and left a note for Mrs Whitehead, our daily help. I had a fairly heavy day, but I reckoned if I took the Tomtit I would have time to exercise Tony, give the ducks and chickens their last meal, have a bath and change and then get the car out in time to reach the hospital before blackout. The Tomtit was ticking over as I stepped from the last Spitfire and I jumped into the cockpit, opening the throttle to take off due west from the hangar apron. I had done so many times before, as the soft re-seeded ground did not worry the light aircraft. I remember glancing at my watch and thinking I could just make it when everything exploded around me. I struggled to wake up and groped for the bedside light, thanking God that it was only a nightmare and time to get up and bathed. As I struggled to clear the haze with which my mind was clogged, the horrible truth slowly dawned upon me that this was not a nightmare but awful reality. By that time the ambulance had reached me and all I could think of was getting to Barbara, so I mumbled to

Hargreaves who had come up with the ambulance to get me a car at once. He said something about lifting me into the ambulance and as he tried to restrain me I made a swipe at him and collapsed.

By the time I was conscious the factory doctor, Doctor Waters, had arrived and I was surrounded by my pilots and Flight Shed personnel. I did not know how badly I was hurt, but I felt my throat was swelling up rapidly and beckoned to Doctor Waters to come nearer to me. I pointed to my throat and whispered that I was rapidly having trouble breathing. He examined me quickly and then shouted to a nurse to bring his instrument case and that he would have to insert a tube in my throat until I arrived in the hospital. Apparently I had taken off with one of the parked Spitfires directly in my path and just as I was about to become airborne I had hit it head on with a God-Almighty crack. The tales from the Flight Shed fellows afterwards were quite amusing. Everyone had seen me take off and were silently hypnotised as they watched speechless the Tomtit rapidly approach the unoffending Spitfire. On impact the Tomtit seemed to disintegrate. Everyone was still frozen to the ground, then after what seemed minutes there was a slight movement amongst the rubble and slowly between the torn wings and the shattered airframe and engine I emerged, staggering and holding on to the wreckage for support. As if a signal had been given apparently everyone then leaped into action. As luck would have it I was not badly hurt, but my head had been gashed across the forehead, and as the surgeon concerned told me, it would take sixteen stitches to put it together again. I half joked with him saying he had better make a good job of the sewing or my wife would play hell.

I tried to put on a brave front for such a stupid, humiliating mistake, but I felt very low indeed. I was not so much concerned with my own injuries, but to know Barbara was in another hospital and we could not see each other was a bitter pill to take. Also I was shaken, not by what had happened so much, but as to why it had happened. I always prided myself on being reasonably clear minded and alert, as in fact most pilots had to be if they wanted to stay alive, and I was more upset than I dared admit over the fact that I had not seen the parked Spitfire. I would certainly not have taken any machine off unless I could see clear ahead and I can only assume that I was looking forward over the portside and did a slight turn as I swung from the tarmac apron to the right and that the parked aircraft was blanked from my view either by the Tomtit engine or the wing struts. Becker and Dick were most sympathetic over it all and Dick in particular most concerned as Dorrie had been over to see Barbara and had come back very distressed. Both Becker and Dick said it wasn't my fault as the machine shouldn't have been parked on the aerodrome, but as I said to them, I ordered the aircraft to be dispersed there, I knew they were there, and I should have seen them there; there was no one to blame but myself. The Tomtit was a write-off and the Spitfire needed a new fuselage and port wing.

When I came out of hospital Barbara was already home and I felt fine, except my eyes were a little slow in focusing. I returned to work immediately and was surprised when Dick rang up and said, 'I think we're in trouble, Alex. Anderson and Becker tell me you should have had an RAF medical check before flying and Anderson, the Commercial Manager is particularly worried as at the moment the firm's insurance policies may be invalidated.' I said I was quite willing to go to the RAF centre at Halton for a medical checkup when an appointment could be made and in the meantime to set Anderson's mind at rest I would telephone Captain Lamplugh, the head of British Aviation insurance as I knew him very well, and ask what the legal position would be. When I rang Lamplugh he said, 'I know you're not a fool, Alex, and wouldn't fly if you didn't feel OK. I'm happy for you to carry on as you are doing and go for a medical check as soon as it can be arranged.'

We had King Haakon and the Duke of Kent to visit us before I had my medical and just to show the doubting Jonahs that I really was OK I put a little more effort into my flying than usual. The pilots were presented of course and Lowdell, Shepherd and Jicha had done the formation flying, whilst I had done the usual individual aerobatics. It all went off extremely well and Tom Ashton, the new Commanding Officer of the Castle Bromwich RAF who had taken over from Squadron Leader Modley, came over afterwards and said, 'I never believed Modley when he said he had to have a good stiff drink before he watched the flying here, and then another one afterwards. Now I understand.'

I had my medical at Halton about a week later and was passed fit.

THE SUMMER of 1942 saw us start with a series of bad engine failures, which was not particularly good for morale. I had recently had three in a row: a glycol tank fracture and a seized engine; an oil failure; and then something unknown to date which was to become known as the skewgear failure. We were to have many before the cause of the trouble was found. I became so conscious of this that I held my breath when taking off over the factory roofs. I examined every local stretch of good road, which might make a possible forced-landing strip, and polished up my dead-stick landing technique by diving on to the edge of the aerodrome at high speed, cutting the throttle and landing without having either crossed the boundary line or exceeding 50 ft in height as I swung the machine into a series of low high-'G' fast vertical banks to throw off my speed rapidly before snapping the flaps and under-carriage down for a landing off one of the turns. I did not always get it in as well as I would have liked but it was certainly good practice for engine failures, and I was lucky to have a comparatively deserted airfield like Castle Bromwich in which to practice. These skewgear failures were more disturbing because there was no warning of any kind and they often occurred after a machine had been climbed, dived at full throttle, tested and probably had several landings and adjustments.

My first happened at Cosford in EP499 when I had completed the machine and was about to turn back to the aerodrome for the final landing. As I flew at normal power and revs the engine suddenly stopped as if the magnetos had been switched off. It took me by surprise, I had not much height and had to look around quickly. I chose an arable field which appeared to be recently harrowed and, with the tense concentration that is required at such moments, I cleared the boundary hedge with a nice margin, put the flaps down and the belly of the machine hit the dry, loose earth in a cloud of dust that obliterated all view for a few moments. When the plunging machine had come to a standstill I stepped out well pleased that I had chosen a good place.

I used to think a Spitfire would fly through anything and only once do I recollect a machine being damaged to a point where it became unserviceable in flight. I see from my log book that it took place on 18 May 1942 and the record runs: 'EN970. This machine was flown for twenty minutes, the weather was bad and the climb completed to 19,000 ft in rain, ice and hail. As a clear space could not be found in the cloud to complete the trials the machine was dived to 460 IAS, and on landing all the leading edge surfaces had been stripped to the bare metal, the fabric gun covers torn away, and the Rotol airscrew was on the point of breaking up as all paint had been removed and the metal gauze protective covering had been exposed and torn so that the resin was breaking away from the now unprotected laminations. It was obvious that the machine had only been landed just in time.'

On 17 June in EP353 I had another skewgear failure at Desford. This time I had climbed to 17,500 ft and after fifteen minutes started to dive and at 460 I eased the throttle back and on opening up again found the engine dead as mutton. After a little careful manoeuvring in between the Tiger Moth training machines I was able to land on the airfield with wheels and flaps down and was also able to tell our ground staff, rather more casually than I really felt, that it was only another skewgear failure.

I seemed to be having most of these failures but when Ulstad had one and ploughed through an enormous hedge, which saved him, and then Squadron Leader Ellis did a belly landing in a ploughed field, I thought it was about time I placed on record my views to Rolls-Royce concerning these failures in no uncertain terms. I ended by saying that unless the cause could be found it would not be long before one of our pilots was killed in the resulting forced landing.

On 24 June in EP437 I had yet another skewgear failure and this time again I was lucky to be able to glide back to Castle Bromwich and land without further damage. My prophecy to Rolls, however, almost came true on 18 July in EP615. I had taken this machine over to Cosford on a test in order to do the first flight on another Spitfire awaiting flight trials over there. The machine I took was perfectly OK but as I landed I felt the starboard wing stall slightly at about three to five mph higher than it should have done and I made a mental note to have the camera door fastened and sealed as this was obviously the cause. Unfortunately, something cropped up suddenly as I stepped from the machine and I forgot to tell our Cosford mechanics to deal with it. After about an hour I had cleared EP510, the Cosford machine and set off in EP615 for Castle Bromwich. The cloud was about 800 ft and ten-tenths and as I was tired and it was the last flight of the day I did not shoot up into the cloud, but decided to return leisurely below in clear conditions. I was just thinking that Barbara and I could pick some of our wonderful strawberries and new potatoes for supper that evening if there were no snags at Castle Bromwich, when suddenly without a spit or cough the engine stopped and I was in an awful, ominous silence, other than the noise of the slipstream which slowly died away as the machine went into a normal glide. I looked below in desperation but all I could see in that depressing black countryside was steelworks, electric pylons, terraced houses and the odd highly banked canal. For a split second a wave of uncontrollable panic surged through me. On reflection I do not honestly think this was due to the knowledge of the possible consequences, so much as the fatal decision I was forced to make. It was Russian Roulette with a double-barrelled gun but both barrels were loaded. I could bale out, but would I make it? I could try to put the machine down—but where—and would I survive? I didn't want to make the final decision but in the seconds I had to spare I was compelled to act and to do it instantly. Once I had decided on my course of action I became calm but I felt in my heart that this was my last flight. I must at all costs avoid the foundries and factories and for the same reason the compact rows of terraced houses. I chose a small gap in between two rows of houses on which were garden sheds, vegetable plots and the odd few yards of lawns, with a small paddock in which were a few solid-looking trees. At the end of the rows of houses was a canal and I reasoned that if the cabbages and garden sheds did not bring me to a standstill, the canal banks certainly would. In the last few seconds as I sat in the machine for the final turn I prayed hard. I hoped above all that Barbara would not be hurt too much, particularly when she had to identify me; I knew my father would be hit badly but he would have pride in the fact that I had done the job to the best of my ability. My final movements were to pull on the Sutton harness with all my strength so that the straps cut into my shoulders and then to lower the seat to its lowest position so that I could barely see out of the cockpit. Just at the most critical stage when concentration was at its highest I was about to congratulate myself on having hit off the exact spot on the vegetable row when the starboard wing stalled, fell away, and I remembered with extreme bitterness the fact that I had forgotten about the camera door.

Everything was now in the hands of God: as the machine snaked off to the right the starboard wing caught a large oak tree and snapped off like a carrot; the nose then swung into the house whose cabbage plot I had tried to take over, the engine tore a gaping hole, exposing the kitchen furniture to wholesale view. As the airscrew dropped onto the floor the port wing plunged into the soft ground and it also snapped off, the unrestricted fuselage then tore through everything in front of it and the earth, vegetables and debris flew up over the cockpit in which I still remained in a terrifying crescendo. I prayed silently that it would all be over soon without too much pain.

The blunt nose of the cockpit bulkhead must have struck something hard for it suddenly lurched over and round, tearing the fuselage in half just behind where I sat, but as it poised to bury me upside down it suddenly hung for a split second or so and then fell back and there was dead silence. I was in a dazed condition; I then saw the blood trickling down my left hand, the arm felt numb and I guessed it had broken. My legs and thighs hurt like hell and I daren't look at them to see how mangled they were. Blood was also trickling into my mouth. I was grateful to God that I was alive and I reasoned that I should not move, but wait until I could be cut out and given some morphia. I must have remained quiet and still for several minutes, closing my eyes as I became conscious of my injuries. I heard running water and thought of the canal; in my bemused state I slowly reasoned that I was some distance from the canal and then as my senses slowly cleared I was appalled to see petrol cascading all over me and to realise that the smell was becoming overpowering. In a flash I thought, 'Oh God, this bloody thing is going up in smoke any minute and I am going to be roasted alive.' In panic I instinctively undid my parachute and Sutton harness, pulled on the cockpit hood release lever and in split seconds I was out of the cockpit and onto the beautiful firm earth. When I realised the machine was not going to burst into flames it came to me with joy and relief beyond measure that there I was standing on my own two feet. I couldn't believe it. I felt first my head, then my arms and then in a mad-like frolic tried my legs. I was bruised and cut a bit but really considering all, I was barely scratched.

As I sat on the remains of the cockpit in an elated mood of contemplation I heard someone running, shouting and crying at the same time, I looked up and a poor hysterical woman was, between the bouts of weeping, asking me how many more of my crew were in the aircraft. I said not to worry, I was sorry about her house if that was it, but I was alone and unhurt. Just then a man came out with a cup of tea in his hand, shaking so much that there was not much left by the time he got to me; what a welcome drink that was but as I put it to my lips—I did not drink in those days—the awful smell of brandy with which the tea had strongly been laced, nearly made me retch. I smiled at the white, trembling man, who had been so thoughtful and kind and said, 'I'm sorry sir, but I don't drink alcohol, and in any case I think you really need it more than I.' With that he bolted the tea down hurriedly and ran inside to make me another cup.

I was late home but this caused no comment from Barbara, who was used to it. She told me she had been busy as she waited for me and had cut the large lawn, picked the strawberries and as soon as I had had a bath, the supper would be ready. Usually Barbara would come up with a cup of tea and sit on the edge of the bath and talk for a while, but this evening I knew she would be busy with the supper. I had just soaped up, however, when she came in with a drink. I hoped the soapsuds would cover my marks and bruises as I never let her know when I had had a forced landing if I could help it. We started to chat and then she blurted out, 'My God, what have you done to yourself?' I said, 'Nothing much; I put a Spit down in a hurry and my harness was too loose.' When years later she saw the photographs, she couldn't speak.

I think Dick must have taken my views to heart, as we began to use the spare Flight Shed blocks and any men not on immediate jobs with Spitfires for assembling repaired Wellingtons. On 31 July we flew our first machine on test. On 14 August I had another skewgear failure on EP955. I was between Elmdon and Castle Bromwich, but as the balloons were down I thought I could make our own airfield; even though the wind was against me from the north, it was not very strong. As I cleared the boundary running parallel with the Flight Sheds I lowered the flaps and undercarriage and in a mixed mood of elation at getting down safely and bitter anger against these engine failures, I slammed the machine onto the hard ground, jammed on the brakes as hard as I dare and swung round in a cloud of dust almost onto the flight apron. Billy Buckley came rushing over with Hargreaves as they knew something must be wrong and when I said, 'Another skewgear, Billy,' he replied, 'My God, another machine saved. And there's Brown over there from the technical office and he had the temerity to say it was a bloody awful landing.'

Some of the fellows in the Flight Shed were beginning to look a bit jaded: Eric Holden had been ill, Billy suffering severe pains in his buttocks from the sciatic nerve and many others that I knew looked drawn and tired. I was then told that many were on nearly every other night fire-watching. When I looked into it I found they were only a small proportion of the men who were actually down for this duty. I worked it out; if we all did a turn it would not be a real hardship to anyone, so I issued an instruction that everyone, starting with me, would do fire-watching duty unless they could put forward good reasons for not doing so. I hated my spell but like the others I only had to do it about once a fortnight; it was a fairly easy chore. One man, however, would not co-operate and when he came to see me I tried to be fair and reasonable and listen to his point of view. He was a conscientious objector and as they did not get paid for the fire-watching, he was not going to do it. I said, 'Every man is entitled to his own point of view, but in my opinion I feel we have a very easy life here; we are well paid, we get home every night, we see our wives and families; many of us have relatives and friends who are in the firing line who would have jumped at the chances we had. So I thought the least we could do was to pull our weight the best we could.' This made no impression at all. The man said, 'I'm not going to do it and you can't make me.' I said sharply, 'If I had the power I would put you in the army now and then I think you would change your mind quickly enough, but as it is I don't want to see you here again.' He started to tell me I couldn't move him, so I called our Vickers police over and he was put outside the gates. Later that day, Bernard Cook, the Works Manager, rang me up and said, 'The man you fired has been to see me and has demanded to be reinstated.' He was in a difficult position with the union. I said, 'I'm sorry, that's your problem; but I will not have that man on this aerodrome again.' How it was settled I do not know, but I never saw the man from then on.

As a result of my forced landing at Willenhall in the black country, there was now tremendous pressure brought to bear in an endeavour to find the cause of the skewgear trouble. As I was the only pilot out of several who seemed to be getting the majority of these failures, one might have thought this was due to pilotage and operation in some form or another; but Rolls ruled this out as a complete impossibility. Of course when I thought about it, it was a matter of mere mathematical statistics: I flew more aircraft than most of the pilots and therefore it was only to be expected that I should receive most of the failures. All of the experts from Lord Hives down were, however, pursuing the matter with unusual vigour. I say unusual because in the past I had often resented the superior attitude of some of the Rolls-Royce personnel, although there were of course amongst them some very good friends of mine, who were serious and extremely capable technicians. I suppose the Merlin will go down in our history as the finest engine we have ever produced in such prodigious quantities, just as the Gipsy engine will for light aircraft. It is, however, nonsense just because you have provided the best engine in the world, to get imbued with an attitude of mind that nothing can possibly go wrong with it.

My records show 127 forced landings were made at Castle Bromwich in the six years I was there. They may not all have been due to engine failure but most were and they ranged from bale-outs to a simple oil-pressure failure. They occurred in Wellingtons, Lancasters, Spitfires and Seafires, and took place on Merlin and Griffon engines. If anyone wants the information I can supply the exact date, almost the exact time and give the precise details of each breakdown, the number and type of machine and where it took place. I have no doubt that if more pilots had been killed, as they might well have been in such a congested area as the Midlands when an engine failed, more would have been made of them. As it is, they are merely insignificant records on the files that no one ever reads. But I get a little angry if I ever hear anyone trying to embroider over these unpleasant facts.

On 20 September I had a change from the almost noiseless skewgear failures. I had almost completed trials on Spitfire AD272 when on a level run at 10,000 ft at maximum power and full revs, the engine misfired and almost at the same time volumes of smoke and steam cascaded out of the engine cowling. I snapped the throttle back but the windmilling airscrew threatened at first to tear the engine out of the frame. I slowed the machine to a stall, the propeller stopped windmilling and the engine seized solid so that all was quiet and peaceful except for the plume of smoke that continued to belch for a while from the side of the engine. I was within reach of the airfield and the weather was good, so that I was able to land normally in front of almost all of the Flight Shed men, who had been warned by either Hastings or Buckley that I was in trouble, and that surprisingly my propeller had stopped. I guessed the engine failure to be caused by piston seizure. When the cowlings were removed one could see the gaping hole in the crankcase torn open by the con-rods and even at that stage I was not sure.

In October of that year we started a series of airscrew failures. It had nothing to do with the engine, but they were just as disastrous. The hydromatic valves in the airscrew we were using would suddenly go into coarse pitch and stall the engine to such an extent that it had to be switched off. I had the first of these failures in ER643 at 18,000 ft. I was a long way from Castle Bromwich and on the way down in a noiseless glide I had plenty of time to determine which aerodrome to choose. It was a bind having a car sent out any distance so I concentrated carefully on making it back home. There was little or no wind and I was able to touch down intact, without damage. I wondered what the new problem could be this time.

Early in October Becker came over and asked how I felt

about finishing another firm's work. I said, 'It all depends. What have you got in mind?' He said that Boulton Paul at Wolverhampton had constructed a 170-gallon drop tank and a service Spitfire had been supplied to do the trials, but there was trouble between the management and the pilots, so that their pilots had refused to fly. I said, 'Well, I don't want to get involved in their troubles, but provided I can ring them up and tell them how I feel I will certainly do the job.' I rang up their chief test pilot and apparently the trials called for a first flight with the tank empty, to land at Llanbedr on the coast of Wales; a take-off with the tank filled with water, a check on the take-off time; a series of brief trials on full load and then a flight over the sea where I was to jettison the full tank making sure beforehand that no shipping was in the way. Llanbedr was a lonely isolated aerodrome only used I think occasionally by Coastal Command. I flew the cumbersome Spitfire with its enormously inflated belly there from Wolverhampton and awaited the tedious process of filling it up from a small water hose. The take-off was better than I expected and having carried out all the required tests over the sea, I swung round in a few tight turns to see if I could trace the wake of a ship and then gave the release lever a hard pull. As the lightened machine lurched away I watched with fascination as the ugly tank cavorted slowly over and over to plunge with a splash into the sea below.*

Dick rang up about that time to say he was coming over to my office with Becker, a Ministry of Aircraft Production representative and the Manager of the contracting firm, Douglas and Co. He wanted to discuss the runway to be installed so that we could test the Lancasters now in the course of production at Castle Bromwich. As they trooped into my office survey maps were brought out and a lengthy discussion took place in which I had very little to say. All I could see was that with so much work to be carried out, I doubted whether

* I learned afterwards that these tanks were used in supplying replacement Spitfires to Malta by air. For a further account see Alfred Price, *Spitfire, A Documentary History* (London, 1977), pp. 95–9.

they would get it done in time for the first Lancaster, which was due for flight trials in six month's time. As Becker and the others were going over the position of the perimeter tracks and main runways, Dick said to me, 'You know, Alex, it seems an awful lot of money to spend; especially when the aerodrome will not be used after the war.' I said, 'Well, they are not spending their own money. If I had my way we wouldn't put in any perimeter tracks or runways at all, but just a tarmac road up to the centre of the field and then to make sure we do not churn the grass up too much, maybe a runway 400 to 500 yards in length for the initial start and touch down on landing.' He said, 'Do you really mean that?' I said, 'Of course I do.' He replied, 'Well, it would certainly save an awful lot of money.' When the others came back Dick said, 'My chief test pilot says all this work is unnecessary just for the Lancaster contract, and he proposes a small linking road running from the Flight Shed apron with a short runway of 400 to 500 yards long.' I gathered at once that I was not over popular. The contractors pointed out how soft and sticky the land was and both Becker and the Ministry of Aircraft Production representative said how serious it would be if we couldn't operate. Dick looked at me and I knew I was in a tough spot as he said, 'You're the only one to decide Alex. After all, you've got to fly them.' I said, 'I am prepared to bank my reputation on it.' For years afterwards people would say as they visited Castle Bromwich, what a stupid thing to do, just to put a short strip of runway on the edge of an airfield and leave it to finish in the middle. From my point of view it did the job more than adequately and the taxpayer was better off by several hundred thousand pounds.

We were having a real spate of airscrew trouble at that time and I had had a number which had either gone into coarse pitch or worse still, into fine which nearly always over-revved the engine to such an extent that it blew up. On 2 October in ER660 I had I think my last skewgear failure, but very nearly ran into complete disaster as I tried to put the machine down. I had gone south of Castle Bromwich in the direction of

Warwick and I could see for miles: our house, The Ridings, showed up clearly between Meriden and Hampton-in-Arden. As the machine had had all the adjustments completed the only thing left for me to do was a full-throttle dive; I commenced it over Kenilworth and passed over Elmdon aerodrome sufficiently high to avoid all the Tiger Moths that filled the sky like wasps round a jampot. Almost at the bottom of the dive without a cough or sound I sensed that the skewgear had gone. At first I could not believe it: the boost was at twelve pounds, the revs at 3000 and the oil pressure 90 lb, which was normal; but of course as I pulled up and lost speed so everything fell back until there was silence broken only by the airscrew still windmilling slowly and the slipstream hissing over the cockpit hood.

I stuck to my original course so that I could put down at Castle Bromwich but suddenly I realised that the balloons were up and poised in the sky and that any small detour to miss them might leave me short of Castle Bromwich to land in the sewage farm adjoining the airfield. I looked at the road from Elmdon to Coleshill and had almost decided to attempt a landing on it when I saw a convoy of army lorries taking up most of the sector which I wanted to use. I had to make up my mind quickly if I was going to use Elmdon as I had only just enough height to reach it. I could see five or six Tiger Moths making their final approaches at the same time and many others on a left-hand circuit. I waggled the Spitfire wings rapidly from side to side in the hope that the Control Officer at Elmdon would see me and realise that I was in trouble and fire a red Very light to warn the Tigers, but nothing happened as I manoeuvred among the machines for landing. Just as I had things nicely set with a Tiger Moth on my starboard side and one a little below which I was about to overtake, I was shaken to notice another Tiger almost underneath me and on my port side but closing in with the other Tiger so that I either had to go over the top of them or quickly dive underneath; if I went over the top I knew I should lose sight of them both and although my gliding speed was much higher my rate of descent was also much greater and I could collide easily without seeing them. I left it until I was looking at the instruments of the Tiger to the right of me and cursing madly, pushed the nose of the Spitfire down, doing an S-turn at the same time to miss them. I then found myself with too much speed and right over the one and only runway Elmdon possessed. I thought for a while that I should overshoot and left my undercarriage up whilst I frantically threw the machine from right to left to throw off my surplus speed. When I saw I was not going to finish up on the main Coventry–Birmingham road I pulled the emergency undercarriage lever down and came to a standstill, which left me but a very short walk, with my parachute, to the control tower. When I got there the Austin Motor Company pilot came out to meet me with the Commanding Officer and said with a grin, 'What's happened Alex, did the elastic break?'

I note from my log-book that I flew the first Mark IX produced at the Castle Bromwich works during March 1943. I think it would be fair to say that this was the period when the poetry of R. J. Mitchell's genius began to fade—but only in looks. This was due, not so much to the design alterations in the Spitfire but rather to the remarkable improvement in the output of the new Merlin. This was the Series 61 and 66 which was on the drawing board as far back as my Weybridge days. Mutt Summers had tried to persuade me to stay, offering as bait the new Wellington that Rex Pierson, the Chief Designer, was working on: it was to have a pressurised cockpit and with the projected Merlin 61s it was expected to operate as high as any fighter of that day and be beyond the range of any German defences. I think the main breakthrough in the design of this engine came with the two-stage blower and also the fact that we were now using 100-octane fuel, 20 psi boost and an output of 1550 hp at 11,000 ft and 1370 hp at 24,000 ft. As can be seen there were tremendous technical developments over a comparatively short period of time. Many of course were of a minor nature but, when added all together, the difference between the old Merlin III Series and the one now fitted in the Spitfire Mark IX was immense. The two-stage blower with its after-cooler between the supercharger and the cylinders put it ahead of the latest German designs and gave us a lead we never surrendered. This was again providential, for just as the Mark I and II Spitfires had done so much to win the Battle of Britain the new Spitfires with the Merlin 61s could operate against the Nazis' wonder-fighter the FW 190 with at least a sporting chance of success.

The new engine necessitated fitting a new cooling radiator under the wing and also extending the nose by nine inches. I also seem to recollect that longitudinal stability problems were creeping in and that the tail was modified. However, in spite of this, it still looked very much like the original masterpiece. Its performance as a weapon of war was better but, sad to say, I felt the superb classic flying qualities of the old Mark II were being slowly eroded. These personal views could be discounted immediately when I realised I could now take a machine for a monthly full-performance check as high as 46,000 ft; I could now go to 33,000 ft in less time than the Mark I could go to 19,000 ft, in spite of an increase in weight of over 2000 lb; and the top speed at 22,000 ft was 45 mph faster. I was more than ever impressed on my first flight in the lighter Mark VIII; fitted with the 61 as opposed to the 66 Series, it went even better with 420 mph at a height of just over 26,000 ft.

As I thought of the days, long past, when the superb talents of R. J. Mitchell and his team had put England to the supreme test for speed in the air with the development of the S4, S5 and S6—I felt the wheel had turned the full circle, for Jeffrey telephoned me and said I must come over and fly one of the Spitfires on which they had just fitted floats. This was a flight I was looking forward to, but unlike nipping down to Worthy Down, High Post or Eastleigh, which could be done very quickly, this would take at least a full day to fit everything in. With the work pressure at that time being so heavy I foolishly put the date off until I was in a frame of mind to enjoy it to the full. As so often happens, I put it off until it was too late and never flew the one Spitfire I am sure I should have liked most of all.

Jicha had a forced landing at Castle Bromwich during that time because as he inverted a Spitfire some of the metal filings and general swarf which had not been cleaned out of the fuselage after the final assembly fell into the chassis control mechanism and his undercarriage would not come down. It happened one day when I was on leave at home and Jicha had flown around for a long while, using up fuel and making strenuous attempts to lower the undercarriage. When these failed he landed on his belly alongside the ambulance and firetender. I was told at once about it by Eric Holden on the telephone and said, 'I thought Jicha was on two days' leave.' Eric replied, 'Yes, I think he was, but he decided to come in.' When Venda came in to see me he expected sympathy and understanding, but I went down his throat in no mean manner. 'What the hell do you mean coming in here to fly, when you should have been off duty?' I stormed. 'Don't you know if you won't take your leave then the other pilots feel they can't take theirs? The next time you disobey my instructions it will be your last.' Poor old Venda was utterly dejected and I was immediately sorry for my outburst. I said, 'Forget it, it could have been worse and in any case it wasn't your fault. I have told them for years there would be a serious accident if they didn't clean the swarf out of the machine before flight.' I then told him of one of my earlier tests when, during a dive, the control column jammed. I couldn't get out because I was diving too fast, and in desperation pulled on the elevator control with all my strength. I felt something give way and came out of the dive OK. When the inspector examined the control system they found that a $\frac{1}{4}$-in. bolt had jammed in the elevator assembly unit near the tail and when I had heaved on the column this had drawn the bolt through, leaving a deep score-mark in the metal.

I think I must have been getting very stale about this time as it was affecting my temper and I would dearly have liked to have packed the job up. Although I could not tell Barbara, I felt inwardly that if I was going to be killed, I would rather do so fighting than in a dull grind of a job with which I was heartily sick. I decided to get away to Boscombe Down for a few days, fly some different fighters and bombers and talk to a few different people. I had a peculiar experience which worried me a little as I could not understand it. On this particular day there was thick heavy cloud although the weather was not too difficult for flying; I had settled down to a steady climb knowing that it would be at least 10,000 ft before clearing the top. As I put down the first set of figures I had the oddest feeling come over me. I felt that part of me was leaving my body and I was looking down at myself. I was so shaken that I closed the throttle and went down below the cloudbase. In a few minutes I felt perfectly normal and went up again to complete the climb. Again I had this most extraordinary feeling, just as if I was a person within a person and that I had left my body and was looking on in some detached manner. It took all my willpower to carry on, but again when running into the bright blue sky above I quickly returned to normal. I never mentioned this to a soul and I never experienced it again, but at the time I thought I was going to have a breakdown of some sort and if I mentioned it to the doctor I should be laid off.

I never consciously worried about the forced landings we were having. I have no doubt I was afraid at the time like any other normal person, but I was I think mentally and physically fit, on top of my job as I had never been before, and with the hundreds of aerobatic shows I had to give, I felt no one could sense the behaviour of a Spitfire better than I. I was very confident of myself and although not religious I had great faith—faith in what I am not quite sure; just that given a chance I felt I could come out OK. But we had so many near do's in that period that I must have thought my luck could

not last for ever. I got tired more easily. I
factors: noise and excess 'G'-loadings as a
aerobatic displays. Although I had never 'blac
aerobatic demonstrations, which for me would
normal seating position and at times probably we
7 'G', there were of course higher load factors im
normally would have been the case and a high degre
centration was necessary. Funnily enough the worst case of
blackout I ever had was at a very low 'G'-loading. It took
place at Desford. As I looked down at the cloud beneath,
there was a clear hole through which I could see the aerodrome,
and I wondered in passing if I could spiral the Spitfire down
this long column without entering the cloud itself. I closed the
throttle and had to keep the machine in a vertically banked
glide with the nose well down. I had an accelerometer on board
and we were building up to just over 2½ 'G'. I kept this up for
some time as we spiralled steeply down and then suddenly I
was blacked out completely. I came to as if I was in a fit, with
my head jerking uncontrollably. I was badly shaken and was
thankful the cloudbase was high, as when I recovered I was in
clear air with Desford aerodrome a few hundred feet below.

Sometimes the development flying was also a little trying. I
occasionally got severe pains in my elbow joints at heights
above 40,000 ft and always a severe headache if I was up for
several hours at a time on some tedious job at heights as low
as 10,000 ft and I had not bothered to use oxygen. I found a
cure for this later on, however, as not only would I use oxygen
from 5000 ft up on long bomber tests, but if I had a headache
would take a breath or two of pure oxygen and as a rule this
would do the trick. I think another psychological problem,
which I may not have appreciated at the time, was the lack of
results and satisfaction at my job. The job of production testing
is really that of a flight inspector; the pilot has to ensure that
everything functions as it is designed to do. The only satisfaction to be achieved is the diagnosis of a fault, at which one
should become fairly proficient if one has enough practice. The

was important inasmuch as greater risks could be taken
with production machines than, say, with a prototype; but
this was up to the pilot and while it may have given him
satisfaction at the time, he also had the dubious distinction of
taking unnecessary risks or even being foolhardy. Development
work was more rewarding in some ways and more frustrating
in others; I found it easier to work with Jeffrey on development
programmes where we would discuss the project with the
design staff for days and weeks beforehand, chew the problems
over as to the type of schedule and tests to be carried out; we
were able to sleep and think on it. At Castle Bromwich when
development work was sent up to me or when I went down to
Worthy Down or Hursley Park, I found it difficult to get into
the right mental groove unless I was there for several days
fully absorbing the atmosphere, which to me stimulated the
right sort of thought processes. As against this in some ways I
was happier in the heavy daily grind that was part of Castle
Bromwich. I always hated the long tedious delays when we
often waited for weeks on end for a special job to be prepared
in some types of development work.

We were now getting numerous American civil and service
missions visiting the factory almost weekly. Lord Halifax paid
a personal visit at about this time. Rightly or wrongly I had
always disagreed with his pre-war foreign policy and when
Dick told me of his proposed visit I laid on a formation
demonstration flight and my usual individual show. We were
very much under pressure when he arrived, so that instead of
landing after my performance I went on to Desford and
Sywell. I don't think Dick was very pleased, and when he said
that Lord Halifax was sorry to have missed me I felt conscious
of my bad manners. Men and women from all stations in life
seemed to come from across the Atlantic during this period of
the war. The Japs had struck with their treacherous blow at
Pearl Harbor, we were defeated in a most humiliating manner
at Singapore and the pride of the Navy, *Prince of Wales* and
Repulse had been blown out of the sea. Our backs were now

more than ever to the wall, we were cornered and the mood of many was that of a trapped snarling lion that knew it was going to be killed, but would not die without an effort. Some of the visits we received were of the greatest importance and if not essential were at least worthwhile.

One day, however, I landed and before I stepped from the cockpit a peculiar looking woman dressed in black leather started taking photographs of myself and the machine from every angle. Mr Talamo introduced us when I had taken off my parachute and helmet and she shot question after question at me but before I could open my mouth she answered the questions for me. I stood this for so long until she tried to push me into various photographic poses and then when I ignored her, she said to Mr Talamo, 'Tell your pilot I have government and Ministry of Aircraft Production approval for this visit: these photographs will go in the magazine and all over the United States of America, and if I do not get co-operation I shall report this when I get back to London.' I said coldly, 'Madam, I am here to fly and not to act as a two-bit film star. If you want to do some reporting I suggest you get on with it.' I then turned and said to the General Manager, 'I'm sorry about this, Mr Talamo, but it seems our manners differ somewhat.' With that I stalked off to my office. I was very edgy and my nerves were strained. I may have needed a holiday, or at least a change, but I thought this must be nonsense as we had spent a very pleasant few days in Cornwall during the summer. Barbara and I had travelled down by train with Dick and Dorrie and we had enjoyed a few nights at Tregenna Castle. Dorrie with her indefatigable energy had walked us all off our feet and the second day Dick had to spend in bed to recover. We rode, fished, walked and played croquet so that when we returned to Castle Bromwich I thought that at least I was well set up for the winter.

One day that summer Maurice Summers brought an elderly American round, by the name of Amos Carter. Dick said he was a real VIP in his own country. He was a nice old man and when I had shown him what a Spitfire could do he would not stop talking. He showed me photograph after photograph of himself dressed as a cowboy riding a white horse up the stone steps of the largest hotel in Houston, while he fired off his ·45s. He showed me photographs of an enormous launch that had been given to him as a going away present. Before he left he said, if I could get leave he would arrange with his government to have me flown out and shown everything I wanted to see anywhere in the United States. Of course I thanked him and said it was not possible and I forgot about the incident until years after the war when I was filling up my car at a service station in El Paso. The old gentleman's name clicked in my memory and I said to the attendant, 'Would you know anyone by the name of Amos Carter in Texas?' He replied with a look of surprise, 'Why sure, everyone knows Amos Carter. I guess he just about owned Texas. He died about a month ago.'

One of the top technicians rang me up from Rolls-Royce and said he was sure I should be pleased to hear that they had traced the cause of the skewgear failures. The story he told me was almost unbelievable. Apparently they had traced all the defective engines to one source and here for some reason or another they were assembling the engines in the opposite way to those normally turned out. The conclusion reached was that all gears and bearings were subject to the same clearances and inspections but for some reason it was thought this change in the assembly position reduced slightly the clearance that should have been given to the main skewgear assembly. I said I was delighted to hear this and went on that we were now in the midst of just as many airscrew failures: probably he could help me to solve this one? He was very pleased to tell me that this time it wasn't Rolls-Royce's headache and wished me the best of luck.

Without doubt the skewgear seizures had given us all greater shocks to the nervous system than any other type of engine failure we were to experience. Lulled into an almost complacent attitude sometimes weeks would pass; apprehension with every flight would ease slightly so that we would forget our fears and consider the crisis over. Then unpredictably, sudden and final it would happen. A pilot was indeed lucky if he was in a position, when it occurred, to do anything about it except pray.

I think it was the awful silence that followed which disturbed me most of all. If an engine exploded or misfired, or a con-rod shot through the side of the crankcase; or it had seized up and oil and glycol fumes plumed from the cowlings, I had always a tense excitement. Presumably this released adrenalin which stimulated a deep urge to fight back with everything I had. But it is more than disconcerting to feel that your engine has lost all power in a dive and not to be sure that this is so. All your instruments, at least for a short while, indicate you have full power. It is when the speed drops away that the instruments begin to tell the truth and from a healthy invigorating noise there follows slowly a deathly silence broken only by the whisper of wind over the cockpit and the realisation of what is below.

The skewgear meshes with the magneto drives on the Merlin and on seizure the gears are either stripped or the shaft fractures. The engine then has no ignition and is behaving in exactly the same way as if all switches have been pressed to the off position—but in this case there is nothing one can do about it.

THERE WAS NO BREAK for Christmas. Having spent some time at Boscombe Down I then went over to Woodford where Sam Brown, as chief test pilot for Avro, and Bill Thorne tested the Lancasters. I wanted a thorough briefing on the machine and was prepared to stay until I knew it inside out. Sid Gleeve had recently joined them and he was very surprised when I laughingly said to him, 'Do you remember me as a boy lifting you off the ground when you skidded in the Manx Senior TT race?' He was killed soon afterwards when a Lancaster on test just nosed over in the dive and plunged vertically into the ground. I never heard the facts relating to this accident but I suspect the machine ran away with him. The Lancaster up to speeds of around 360 IAS was longitudinally stable, but then it got progressively nose heavy and could not be held by the control column without the use of the elevator trim tabs. How bad this could get I'm not sure, as I never tested it to its limits, but I nearly had a similar accident later on which made me think Sid's death was caused by this.

There was a tinge of excitement in the air at the Avro works as Barnes Wallis of Vickers had chosen the Lancaster for the Mohne and Eider dam job and we all thought this was the weapon to sink the Japanese navy so that everything connected with the project was hush-hush in the extreme. I was staggered when I paid a visit to my home in Lincolnshire later that year and a local friend said to me that he had seen the aircraft leave for the raid on the dams. Knowing how secret it was I laughed and said, 'I doubt it. Most likely it was one of the raids on Essen.' He then shook me by saying, 'Oh, no.' He knew it was the dam raid because the bomb doors were open and something stuck out below. I couldn't say so but I knew he was right, because this was one of the features of the bomb assembly for the dam raid.

I think possibly one of the problems that subconsciously weighed on my mind during this period was the fact that Barbara was going to have a baby and was going through a most difficult time. In fact she was under the almost constant care of a gynaecologist and we were all concerned as crisis seemed to follow crisis. As things were so difficult a first-class assistant had been engaged, but she was in such demand that she could come only just before the expected confinement and not earlier.

On 14 February Barbara felt queer after tea and went to lie down. I wondered if it could have been the shocks Barbara occasionally received whilst I was away at work, for there were times when the war seemed very close indeed. Barbara was nearly always alone and although our home was not large there was a great deal of room, with the garage, coach-house, loft and stables. I always left her a 20-bore shotgun and a small Browning automatic pistol, so that when the police came round one day to warn of Germans who had baled out and had not been captured, she loaded the 20-bore and sneaked quietly round the outside premises. As she says, she was so nervous that had there been a poor old tramp in one of the stables, she was sure she would have shot him on sight. One day she was mowing the lawn and there were no air-raid warnings when suddenly she heard machine-gun fire and looking up saw a twin-engined bomber going low overhead. She thought how strange that they should have been testing their guns, when to her horror she saw the crosses on the wings. As she says it was a good thirty yards to the house and she reckoned she cleared it in three leaps without her feet touching the ground in between.

She rested a while in bed but soon I heard her call down the stairs to me and when I rushed up it was to be told that our earlier fears had now materialised. I called the doctor at once and he was at the house within minutes; he said it was useless now calling the gynaecologist, the child was on its way six

weeks too early. There are some battles in life that are fought
in the mind and one is helpless and alone. Dr Chrystall only
drank tea and we must have consumed gallons as he and I
waited through the night with the emergency midwife from the
factory doing all she could upstairs. At 2 in the morning after
many false alarms, Dr Chrystall called to me. I went up to
Barbara, who had not uttered a sound, and saw our son for the
first time. There are sometimes rare moments that one holds as
greater than life or death itself, and this was now. To me our
marriage was one and the birth of our son the other. For the
first time since I joined Vickers, I had no thought for my job,
other than to ring Dick and Dorrie to say I should not be in
that day. Sir Stafford Cripps was to visit the factory and he
sent his best wishes when told I could not be present. The first
two weeks were tense: the nurse could not stay, and another
nurse we were lucky to get was not only inexperienced but also
unsatisfactory in other ways. Alex was a wee $4\frac{1}{2}$ lb at birth but
never really looked back in spite of being put under a cold
window in an unheated house in wintertime, when he should
really have been in an incubator. He cried a good deal at first
until it was discovered that all he really needed was meat and
two veg in the form of special extracts. From then on he went
ahead in leaps and bounds.

The pace at Castle Bromwich was increasing rapidly. We
had completed many repaired Wellingtons and we were preparing the Flight Sheds for the Lancasters. Vickers had just
taken over a factory at South Marston near Swindon and it was
intended to produce the Mark 21 and 22 Spitfires in a short
while. The production of the Mark IX was now increasing so
that I was pressed to keep a check on all the pilots' activities
and at the same time fit in a development flying programme at
Worthy Down. The airscrew failures persisted and I had yet
another in JK940 on almost my first Spitfire test after Alex
was born. A constant-speed unit seized after twenty minutes
flying, causing the airscrew to go into coarse pitch and stopping
the engine. I landed back at Castle Bromwich unharmed

except for frayed nerves and temper. I think all of us at that time were a little edgy; the men were working long hours and at times under the most appalling conditions. The new Merlin engines came from Packards and although they were beautifully finished they had cut out one of the machining processes on the piston skirt, the result of which was that on many of the machines one would get one or two distinct thuds as if the engine were about to seize up. Mostly, however, they settled down. Although I seemed to be fated with failures there were no serious accidents to the other pilots, other than to Flight Lieutenant Phillips, who was killed rolling a Spitfire into the ground. I never found the real cause for the accident, but I suspect it was either a loose harness or pilotage error. I had two forced landings in quick succession: when in LZ993 the oil pressure failed and the bearings seized, but I was lucky and got down without damage; on a Spitfire Mark IX, MA233, I had a dead cut just after take-off. I put it down in such a hurry crosswind on the east side of Castle Bromwich airfield that the undercarriage was not completely lowered and the wingtip dug into the ground, swinging the aircraft round, damaging the fuselage and airscrew before coming to a standstill just short of the aerodrome boundary.

At Heston there was a meeting of service chiefs of all the armed forces, including our allies, with many of our Cabinet Ministers and political heads to view the latest fighters, both on the ground and in the air. It was a day out for me as I met once again old friends whom I had not seen since the beginning of the war. It was also interesting to observe and talk with so many high-ranking military leaders whose thinking and direction at this critical phase of the war would determine our destiny for decades to come. I thought the flying was of a very high order and I also thought at the time that I would like to see any other country put on a better show. Jeffrey Quill, Bill Humble, Geoffrey de Havilland flew with a precision and continuity of smoothness that was a delight to watch; I did my best with a demonstration I thought in keeping with the seriousness of the occasion. My first effort, however, went off like a damp squib: I took off, climbed to 4500 ft in about a minute, rolled over into the inverted position to do a vertical power dive when there was an explosion of air and the cockpit hood pulled away from its release gear and was in danger of flying off as it did once before to damage the rudder and tail-plane. I slowed up as quickly as I could and waggled my wings to indicate I was going to land. The whole show was so well timed and organised, however, that as I touched down I saw one of the Blackburn machines take off to fill in my place. The hood did not take long to fix and again with superb precision the marshals and control officers signalled me to take off. It was a very select gathering on Heston airfield that day: not every air firm was displaying and only the chief pilots for the particular aircraft on display were there. As Yoxall, Chief Photographer for the magazine *Flight* said at the time, 'What a field day Jerry would have if he could bomb us now! A major victory over the navies, armies and air forces, and the cream of British aviation wiped out at the same time.' It was almost like a pre-war meeting for me. The pilots who knew each other well went off to the pub at Heston for lunch and we had a lot of lighthearted banter between us. Geoffrey de Havilland said to me, 'Don't set such a bloody high standard, Alex; don't forget we have to follow you.' There was no rancour, and I knew Geoff was paying a very rare compliment as I thought his flying in the Vampire later on was unexcelled by anyone. When I returned to Barbara and Alex that night it was with a feeling of quiet satisfaction that if this was not the beginning of the end it may have at least been the end of the beginning.

As our tempo of work now increased there was a feeling of tense but quiet confidence. Sometimes a lighthearted note crept in as when I did the Spitfire flying at Radcliffe for the film *Ferry Pilot*. Three cameras were set up at suitable focal points on the field and my job was to do a series of low aerobatics in front of them. I thought the shots came out fairly well, but the camera technique of today would have put the whole programme to shame. I also did a series in the Birmingham studios and in the air on the day-to-day work of a test pilot, which seemed well received as I was asked by a magazine for a photographic story on similar lines. The last Wellington was cleared from Castle Bromwich ironically enough with a starboard engine failure, and I flew the first Lancaster, DV272, from the airfield on 16 October 1943; this was not the first production machine but one of twelve machines which we had assembled in the Flight Shed by arrangement with Avros.

On 12 October I had had an experience with Spitfire MJ190 which I kept from Barbara, but it left me pretty shaken. There had been no flying all day owing to fog. In the late afternoon it began to clear, so I said to the other pilots that I did not think much of it but would have a look. Out of habit in bad weather I flew in my own sector almost due north in the direction of Cannock Chase. There was low ground fog in wide areas and the Hams Hall steam plummeted up above it like an Indian smoke signal; there was a layer of stratus cloud at about 8000 ft and as I climbed to 17,000 ft I broke out into beautiful clear sunshine. The machine seemed to be OK so I decided to do one power dive, a full-throttle level run back to the column of steam at Hams Hall, and then land. I was just making a note on my pad as the machine dived towards the stratus below and was about to ease out, when everything seemed to blow up in my face: oil and glycol spewed out of the engine cowling obliterating any view I had through the cockpit; smoke poured out of the starboard side, and the engine was vibrating and shaking so badly that I knew unless I slowed up quickly it would be wrenched from the airframe. This time there was no decision to make, the issue was clear cut. Even if I was able to slow down the machine to stop that destructive windmilling airscrew, I knew that once I broke through the layer of stratus below I would have a job to see the ground and no chance at all of pulling off a landing of any sort. Things were now starting to break away and hit the side of the machine with a terrifying thump and the sooner I got out the better. I thought of scribbling a note to Barbara on my pad in case I didn't make it and then hesitated because I didn't know what to say; in any case I might be over-dramatising the situation, so I scrawled rapidly on my pad, 'Baling out—engine seizure—suspect piston or con-rod.' I had barely finished my scrawl when the machine shook so much that I tore out my safety harness pin, pulled down my goggles to protect my eyes from the oil, glycol and debris, snapped back the cockpit hood and with all my strength kicked myself away from the cockpit. What happened then I am not sure: whether I fouled the machine or struck a piece of engine cowling tearing itself off, I shall never know; I only remember going over and over as I frantically searched for the rip-cord. Finding it, I pulled and after a lapse of a few seconds I felt the terrific snatch of the parachute harness bite into my shoulders and thighs and the safety-lock box pull into the pit of my stomach with such force that I momentarily retched. I could not help thinking of Alex, with his burps and windypuffs. The shock jerked at me with such viciousness that I was amazed to see one of my old beloved flying boots shoot off from my right leg and lazily fall over and over to be lost from view as it penetrated the stratus cloud below. Whether it was the intense relief at finding myself with an open parachute or some instinctive reaction as a result of releasing the parachute for so many, many times on the ground after landing and giving the control box a quick twist and then a sharp blow with the fist so that the harness fell away for me, I shall never know, but the incredible thing is that I had the awful urge when I saw the boot disappearing below to twist the parachute control box and release the harness so that I could catch up with it. For years afterwards there were many times when I would wake up in a cold sweat having dreamt of what would have happened if I had done just that.

I was now in beautiful sunshine, quietly and slowly sinking to the cloud below. I felt in good shape and well pleased with my escape. Then as I looked up into the blue sky above I froze in horror at what I saw: three complete sections of the parachute canopy were missing and the remainder of the chute was held by one single strand of silk, that even from there looked frayed as if it would give way at any moment. My mouth went dry and I remained rigid; not daring to move I watched the single strand of silk as we slowly drifted downwards now out of the brilliant sunshine through the narrow layer of cold stratus cloud; below I saw the widespread belts of fog and way in the distance the long white plume of Hams Hall. When I had time to get my breath and think, I wondered what could have happened to the chute. I wasn't sure when the damage took place; what puzzled me was the fact that at no time did I see any of the silk panels floating away from me. Even if part of the aircraft had broken away as I jumped out and had caught my parachute pack before it opened, I thought I would have seen the pieces falling below in the clear sunshine. But then again I may have been momentarily knocked out, as I do not recollect seeing the machine once I had left it. I decided in any case to push the matter to one side as only two things bothered me at that moment: one, whether the chute would hold together or suddenly plummet me to the ground; or, if it did hold, how hard was I going to hit Mother Earth with only one boot?

As far as I could now see in the haze and fog I was clear of all electric pylons, factories and houses and I guessed I was going to land in marshy farmland near Rugeley. It was dull, calm and quiet as I gently floated down; even my breathing was hushed as I clung onto the harness, willing it to stay in one piece. I was conscious of how cold my right foot was and that I was surprised to hear the cackle of a cockerel down below. I counted the last few feet in terms of survival if the slender frayed silk cord were to break. When less than 50 ft up I carefully unlocked the harness release box and hung by my arms in readiness for the ground, which suddenly came up to meet me at an alarming rate. Both my feet plunged into the marshy mud and I was thrown onto my back, to lie there as if on a soft wet feather bed, so relieved was I to get down safely. No one had seen me land; I was alone and nothing in sight other than a narrow farm track and the large, sticky, muddy field in which I stood. I decided to leave the parachute near the farm road and in a series of hops to follow the road wherever it might lead. After a hundred yards or so in the misty light I saw a cottage and small farmyard. The woman who opened the door as I knocked looked at me with alarm and suspicion but when I had allayed her fears she was more than kind and helpful. Luckily she had a telephone and after getting through to my office, I called a taxi from Rugeley, which arrived in good time. The driver said, however, that he could not drive me all the way to Castle Bromwich as his licence did not permit it and neither did his petrol allowance. I was not in the mood to listen to excuses and said bluntly, 'You get me to Castle Bromwich and quick. I'll see you get some petrol coupons and I will deal with the police if you are stopped.' With that he set to with a will. Dick, some of the management staff and all the pilots and Flight Shed staff were waiting on the apron near my office as the taxi drove onto the airfield. To this day the damage to my parachute remains a mystery. The RAF accidents branch took the damaged chute and, apart from the missing panels, could find nothing wrong with it.

The spirit throughout the whole Flight Shed was marvellous. By this time, keenness and enthusiasm went right through every department, so that now it was not a question of when we should do a job but that we would carry on without stopping until it was completed. There was now never any quibble about late night flying or early morning take-offs. AID got used to me and arranged things so that we got on very well together.

The Lancaster production at Castle Bromwich increased my own work load considerably, but at the same time it did make a great change from the all too familiar little Spitfire. We had now more press visits, overseas missions and VIPs than ever before and I was called upon more frequently to demonstrate not only the latest Spitfire or Seafire but the Lancaster as well.

I realised at the time that I was indeed fortunate, from a flying point of view: not only had I been given the best fighter, but I now also had the best four-engined bomber in the country, and in many people's opinion the two best aircraft in the world at that period. I loved the Lancaster almost as much as I did the Spitfire and in its own way this heavy machine would perform almost as well. It had no vices and I treated it in the same manner as I would a smaller aircraft; I just had to remember to slow up the whole tempo and give the heavy machine time to respond to gentle but firm control. With the small rough airfield of Castle Bromwich surrounded as it was with obstacles of every kind, there was little room for error on landing, but in a very short while I found the Lancaster, with light load, could be placed in an exact spot without difficulty. In fact so often on the approach, after a successful final test-flight, the throttles could be pulled back, the machine put into a number of tight gliding turns and with a few side-slips, put down in very much the manner of a Tiger Moth. In the air, I always felt at home when at the controls, although the enormous size of the cockpit, by comparison with the Spitfire, was demoralising to start with. The control response was slow and ponderous after the rapid movements of the Spitfire but, given time and gentle persuasion, there was little the big bomber would not do. It seemed to me that not only would it execute manoeuvres unusual for a four-engined machine of its size, but it would do them with the utmost grace, smoothness and dignity. If I had any fears about abusing such a remarkable aircraft they were confined to the longitudinal stability at speeds in excess of 360 IAS, and that the rudder-fins could be 'shock-stalled' with 'over-load'.

About this time Lowdell was posted to Weybridge. I was sorry as George had done a good job and I was at the time arranging for him to assist in the Lancaster programme, which was due to start any day. I cannot remember why he went to Weybridge, but I think he was given the chance to fly there and it suited his domestic arrangements better.

I never liked to see too many Lancasters parked waiting delivery, so if necessary I would arrange to deliver them ourselves. Mostly other than the long jaunts to Scotland, they were to such stations as Waddington, Coningsby, Binbrook, Ludford Magna and so on, which we could usefully fit in after the day's work was over. Once I took one to Waddington rather late, and Venda came with the Oxford to pick us up. To make up the crew in the Lancaster I had taken Ossy Snell, Olaf Ulstad, and Jim Rosser with me just for the ride. I took over the Oxford when we left Waddington; the sun had gone down and I could see fog building up in wide patches, although I did not really worry about getting down somewhere, if the worst came to the worst. I started to have a little fun with the pilots. I said to Jicha, 'How many parachutes have we got on board, Venda?' He looked around and there was a chorus of 'Four parachutes, five pilots.' I turned to Olaf with a wink and said, 'I reckon this stuff's going to close in and we may have to jump for it.' Olaf twigged on to my fun at once and he replied, 'Ja, I tink you are right: four 'chutes, five of us—which one stays with the ship?' At that there was a lot of leg-pulling and Venda said, 'The chief must go first, then we do it in order of seniority. You are the junior, Ossy, you must stay with the machine while we jump for it.' 'Jees, you must be joking, the chief and me are married men with responsibilities. You are young and single and no one will miss you; you're the one who has got to stay with the machine,' Ossy responded. The good-natured banter went on all the way to Castle Bromwich, where we were able to land without difficulty. It was a warm, well-knit spirit of comradeship that had built up over the long months of trials and tribulations and it felt good to know that not one of us would have jumped leaving the other behind. It did not have to be put into words.

BERNARD BECKER left Castle Bromwich about this period and we were all sorry to see him go. He had done a good job in a quiet, unobtrusive manner and fitted in very well with the working arrangements both at the factory and at the airfield. His place was taken by a Wing Commander, whom I invited over to have lunch with me and to meet all the pilots. It was going off quite nicely when for some reason or other the conversation got around to our food and shipping problems and the so-called neutrality of Eire. I said the situation was ridiculous and bearing in mind how many wonderful pro-British Irish there were and how many were serving in the forces, I was surprised that something was not done to remove this knife-in-the-back situation. The Wing Commander then said with some bitterness, 'Of course the real trouble with you British is that you've forgotten what happened over four hundred years ago.' There was an awkward silence. I think most of us wondered what on earth he was doing in a Wing Commander's uniform if he felt that way about it. However, he was my guest and with apologies I said he must excuse us as we had work to do.

The matter did not end there. A short while later the Wing Commander started trying to alter our well-established routine by making stipulations about my pilots' dress and insisting on inspecting their logbooks. There seemed to be constant friction between him and the pilots and the atmosphere got gradually worse as the weeks and months went by. The last straw came when he tried to alter the leave rota, most carefully drawn up to ensure fairness to all concerned. In a fury I went over to his office, after warning him on the phone he was going to hear me to his face. He had taken refuge in the Managing Director's office, but that did not deter me: I stormed in and spoke my mind in front of Bonner Dickson. Unbeknown to me, almost everyone in the management block had had their moments with the Wing Commander and Dick had borne the brunt just as I had with the pilots. The factory grapevine had operated so quickly, no doubt through the switchboard when I spoke on the phone, and Reg Leech told me afterwards that he, the Works Manager, and a few others were listening joyfully outside the door which adjoined the management suite. As they said, they hoped and half expected to see one Wing Commander come flying through the glass-partitioned door as the argument got more heated with every word. I never saw the Wing Commander again and neither did the others. From then on peace reigned and we got on with our respective jobs.

Venda Jicha was now a frequent visitor to The Ridings. Beneath the hard, ruthless and sometimes bitter exterior of Jicha, there was a kind, almost pathetic warmth, which came out when he spoke of his sister and parents and when he teased Alex with the beautiful little woolly fawn he had bought him. I felt desperately sorry for him at times: too hard a character to make many friends, suspicious of well-meaning English people, contemptuous of those who could not measure up to his own standards, worried about his family and country and very often much alone. We came as close as I would think it possible for an Englishman to be with a foreigner and we had many laughs together in spite of Venda's misunderstanding of the English type of humour and disgust at it. I had bought Alex a little white Shetland pony called Wendy, which was full of spirit, and I was unable to get anyone locally to tighten up her shoes, which I noticed were loose. I tried to do this myself but found it far from easy. When Venda was over one day I mentioned this and he said, 'It is so easy; I hold the pony in my arms and you take his feet.' I answered, 'I don't think it is as simple as that, Venda; in the first place I do not think you would be able to hold Wendy.' Venda snorted at this and taking off his tunic he went into the stables to pick the pony up in his arms; I stood out of the way by the door, knowing what to expect. Venda made a soothing clucking noise and put his well-built arms around Wendy's shoulders and the next thing I knew was that Venda was flying out of the stable door, flat on his back with Wendy shuffling around indignantly.

Venda lived for flying and he was overjoyed when I promised he could work with me on the Lancaster when it was ready, but that he must do a few runs on and off the nearest good aerodrome before he started to fly them on his own at Castle Bromwich. We had a lot of fun flying together, some of which he did not always appreciate. He was standing beside me in a Lancaster once, by the flight engineer's panel when I said laughingly, 'Why don't you sit on the step, Venda?' He looked at me quizzically and I suddenly eased the control column back to $1\frac{1}{2}$ to 2 'G' and Venda went down on the floor as if he had been poleaxed. Even I was surprised at the way he went down so quickly and of course the rest of the crew roared with laughter. Venda said it was a bloody silly joke.

There was one manoeuvre on the Lancaster that Venda could never stop talking about. It all came about as a bit of devilment: I was flying with a visiting test pilot who had a strong Yorkshire accent and we had done a clean steady power dive to about 360 IAS and had pulled up gently to a stalled turn in an almost vertical bank position when the pilot beside me said, in broad Yorkshire, 'By gum, steady on, chief, or you'll have the bugger over.' This tickled me so much I couldn't resist continuing what seemed to me the smooth completion from the attitude we were now in and I pulled the Lancaster gently but firmly into a positively controlled barrel-roll. From then on it seemed to me perfectly normal to finish off the dive in this manner and the controllability of the Lancaster in a roll was such that I amazed myself more than once by the manner in which a glove, left on top of the instrument panel ledge, could be gently suspended in the air as the machine seemed to roll around it, or if I had a passenger without harness on I was able to go over with his bottom a quarter to half an inch from the seat until we had completed the roll and we were at positive 'G' again. When I did this with Venda he was again standing at my side taking down engine pressures and temperatures and I flipped my hand over to indicate to him that we would do a roll; but he laughed, thinking I was pulling his leg as he had heard the story and did not quite believe it. As we went over and were completely inverted the look on Venda's face was something to be seen: I laughed at him as I gently eased the controls so that his feet left the floor slightly and then settled back—Venda peering out of the cockpit at the ground instead of the sky was something I shall never forget.

Many times I have been asked if rolling a Lancaster put stresses upon the machine for which it was not designed. My immediate reply would be that it depends how the roll is executed. Certainly, I have proved many times that it is possible to roll a Lancaster with no more stress than if it were doing a steep turn. In combat use, a pilot taking evasive action would be expected to impose far greater loads on his machine than I did in a roll that produced no negative 'G' and no more than 1 'G' positive.

Production was now increasing at a most impressive rate and would soon be up to 320 Spitfires a month and about 30 Lancasters, to say nothing of the production at other places, such as South Marston and the development work on exciting projects under Jeffrey at Worthy Down. Since the bombing of Eastleigh and Southampton, Supermarine's had literally been transferred 'lock, stock and barrel' to the palatial mansion and magnificent surroundings of Hursley Park. Here beat the very heart of the Spitfire and here were created all its later progeny. For a relatively small organisation design, test and development (DTD) took place at a prodigious rate.

Although I often visited Hursley Park I was a more frequent visitor to Worthy Down, where I could admire and also fly the originals of this remarkable team. This was usually arranged by a telephone call from Jeffrey to fly the latest new mark. As my logbook now shows, I was asked to carry out DTD work on modified elevators, new design tailplane, stability trials at 40,000 ft plus with modified airscrews; the testing of new type ailerons, trials with redesigned chassis and high-pressure tyres, dives to test the stress factors on the radiator fairings at speeds in excess of 520 IAS and so on. This could be done on almost any mark of Spitfire that happened to be allocated to the DTD group, on a completely new model, or even one altered from the production line.

It was on these occasions that I realised the advantages of having an airfield almost to oneself, as we did at Castle Bromwich. At Worthy Down the Fleet Air Arm were very active training pilots and I was often irritated and concerned when absorbed in a job to be distracted by the constant traffic. Luckily I never had an incident, but Jeffrey landing a Spitfire on the low side of the mound of Worthy Down was suddenly confronted with a Proctor: the Spitfire was scratched a bit but the Proctor written off.

The tempo was such that I was now never sure from day to day just how the programme would go or where I would be. I would sometimes fly the Tomtit from The Ridings, step into a Lancaster awaiting test at Castle Bromwich, land again and take a Spitfire on to Sywell to fly a Wellington; return to take the small works team to South Marston for a conference in the Rapide, Dragon, or Oxford, and then return to Castle Bromwich for more testing. I have been asked in recent years if the change from something like a Tomtit or a Spitfire to a Lancaster made any difference in flying judgement. I have heard some pilots say that it does and that they found the controls uncomfortably light or heavy and that it affected their float-off heights. Personally the only difference I noticed was when I sat in the respective machines and felt the controls, but the moment I opened the throttles or throttle I nearly always felt completely at home.

Jeffrey as always was very helpful to me. One single day of no flying and with such an enormous quantity production we were of course hard pressed to keep up to schedule, so if I rang him up and said we could do with some help, he would send up a few pilots from his own team. Among the many who came up from time to time was Squadron Leader Bartley and Lieutenant Commander Don Robertson. Tony Bartley was a young Fighter Command pilot, ebullient and usually the life and soul of any party. He was married to Deborah Kerr, the film actress, and they were both friends of Dick and Dorrie. I did not see a great deal of Tony as he was attached to Jeffrey's group but he had helped out George Lowdell when I was off-duty with appendicitis. Robertson was a very experienced pilot having been a pre-war Canadian bush pilot, and now seconded from the Fleet Air Arm to be stationed with Jeffrey at Worthy Down. I sometimes felt sorry for the pilots that Jeffrey let me have, as the weather did not always clear too well and they had a tough and uncomfortable stay.

I flew as usual whenever I could and of course by this time I had got the situation in such conditions worked down to a pretty fine art. I also knew the terrain like the back of my hand. If conditions were foggy at Castle Bromwich but clear at any of the other places, which had aircraft awaiting test, I would often use the single taxi-road on the edge of the airfield as a fog line and if the conditions were less than fifty yards would send policemen down the road to control it and signal with a whistle if it was OK for me to take off.

This problem of dealing with so many aircraft when the weather was bad worried me and I became somewhat obsessed with the idea of keeping the flying going under any circumstances. With moderate numbers I had managed in the past but now it was getting beyond me. I decided that the Lancasters were now the most important priority and as they were fitted with beam-landing gear I decided to do a beam-landing course and make suitable arrangements for testing them at a beam-approach aerodrome when conditions were so bad we could not land at Castle Bromwich.

We now had a new overseer, a Wing Commander Gibson,

and I asked him to arrange this specialist course with the blind landing group at Watchfield, near Swindon. 'Hoots' Gibson was a nice friendly person, anxious to be helpful in every way, so the next week I found myself under the type of instruction which both fascinated and challenged me. We did the whole course on Oxfords, except when I was in the Link-trainers. The blind flying side was comparatively easy; after all, as I pointed out to the instructor when they marked the chart 'above average', I had had a little practice over recent years. The actual beam work was also straightforward but I was not too happy about plotting my approach bearings when suddenly given a landing pattern. I realised later that I should have made myself a simple approach indicator, which would automatically have given me the bearings I wanted for any set landing course. (Today my son has a wonderful course and landing-pattern computer that does all this and saves endless mental arithmetic.) However, I came away from the course confident that I should be able to cope adequately, particularly as my final landing was carried out in pitch black darkness without a solitary light to guide us until I had landed, when the aerodrome boundary and runway lights were switched on.

That week when I returned to Castle Bromwich, I nearly had a repeat of my bale out, in a Mark IX, MJ536. This happened on the climb with the boost at 12 lb and the revs at 2850, when at just over 11,000 ft there was a sharp piston thud followed by intense vibration as I snapped the throttle back. Smoke, oil and glycol steam plumed out of the engine cowling so that I could see nothing and the engine threatened to disintegrate from the airframe as I made frantic efforts to try and stop the airscrew from windmilling. I am now looking at the report I made at the time and it reads as follows, 'It is impossible to stop the new airscrews now fitted to the Mark IXs from windmilling by overstalling on engine failure and I recommend that the basic setting on the coarse pitch side be altered, as it is dangerous with some types of engine failures and also the increased drag reduces the length of glide.' By pulling down my goggles, opening the hood and turning without putting my head in the slipstream to be covered in oil, I was able to keep Castle Bromwich in reasonable view and make a landing without further damage, but all the way down I wondered what would happen if the bearers gave way under the violent shaking and the engine suddenly disappeared.

I was in my office one morning when Barbara rang up and in an excited tone told me that there was a letter in from the Chancellery of Knighthood saying that the Prime Minister had been recommended to put my name forward to His Majesty The King to receive an award of the Membership of the British Empire and would I confirm that this would be accepted. I had never given this kind of award the slightest thought until that moment; we were after all doing our job to the best of our ability and I was proud and completely loyal to Vickers. We were the most highly paid pilots in the country and when one worked in an atmosphere of trust and integrity this seemed to me to be enough reward.

The number of employees had now so increased at the Flight Shed that it was almost like a small factory, and yet it never lost its personal intimacy. I'm surprised now to realise that I knew but a handful of men and women by their surnames, and yet I think I would see nearly everyone at some time of the day or other and would know most of them by their christian names. With the tension easing somewhat and the bombing less intense, parties were organised occasionally, and the earliest of these was given to celebrate the birth of Alex. The Flight Shed got together and presented him with a beautiful little silver spoon and pusher and the entertainment that followed made an enjoyable evening in contrast to the usual conditions in which we found ourselves. I decided to make a little buggy-cart or trap on aircraft principles of construction, so Wendy could trot us around the lovely Warwickshire countryside when we had an hour or so to spare. I mentioned this to Eric Holden and he sketched the plan out on his office floor. The job was now to get the materials, which I thought would be most difficult. To my gratification and amazement, however, when I mentioned it to Morris Motors at Cowley as they had spruce and plywood for repairing Moths, the very next day a lorry arrived with more than enough timber and plywood to complete the job. When I asked if I could pay for it I was told it was with their compliments—and anything else I might require. Dunlop sent over a brand-new set of special aircraft wheels complete with tubes and tyres and again would not allow me to pay for them. A young boy, whose name I think was Robert, made very good aircraft models perfect in scale and detail, and he said he would be pleased to make the buggy-cart for me. He had made dozens of models of the various machines that I had flown from time to time; when he started to make the buggy-cart his mother insisted that they clear out their living room so that he had more room in which to work. The whole family I think became involved in the construction and assembly of this beautifully polished piece of work but in their enthusiasm they struck one snag. The work had proceeded to the point where it was ready to fit the wheels and shafts and to their consternation they then realised they could not get the buggy-cart out of the living room: it would not go through the door, nor would it go through the bow window. The mother was adamant, if they had to pull the house down they were not going to damage the buggy-cart. The outcome was that they took out the whole of the bow window frame and with careful manoeuvring they were able to get their precious work out unmarked. It really was a beautiful little cart, smart, highly polished and so light that one man could lift it. We had many happy hours jogging through the country lanes with Alex nestled in Barbara's arms.

It was rare, no matter how much bad weather we had, for me to complete all the stages of tests in complete cloud. Usually there would be layers of different types and often gaps in the layers; there were exceptions, however, and several

Lancasters were flown and tested and cleared without any visual flying except for the take-off and landing. I was more than satisfied with the result and agreeably surprised when I rechecked in clear conditions. With the Spitfire it was not quite the same, I cleared many in such conditions but always liked to put each machine through a short series of aerobatics before I passed it. This led me to practising aerobatics in cloud and I found it more difficult than I had imagined. The most difficult part was to find cloud thick enough to get in such manoeuvres as vertical upward rolls, rocket loops, etc. When I did find the right conditions I was never quite sure whether I was cheating myself or not. I found that if I was reasonably orientated I could roll and loop easily, but when I closed my eyes at the top of a vertical climb to the stall for instance, and when on opening my eyes tried to recover the normal flying position I would more often than not break out of cloud before I had fully recovered. I put in as much practice as I could and with the artificial horizon and the directional gyro always out of action it was amazing how I came to rely upon the turn-and-bank indicator, sensitive altimeter and the ASI as my principal instruments for cloud recovery.

With every week now bringing an increase in production I had to think of delegating more of my own work. The first to be considered was South Marston. We would soon be producing our first Mark 21 and the production on other models justified a full-time pilot who could be resident there. The problem was who to appoint to this not unimportant job. I had with me at the time a Flight Lieutenant Johnson, formerly a school teacher from County Durham. Johnson was a clear-cut blue-eyed man, with fair hair; intelligent, conscientious and loyal. He was the son of a mining family, a confirmed socialist and inclined to show the occasional chip on the shoulder as a result of his hard and austere upbringing. We would discuss the problems of Johnson's childhood and the miserable state of his family in those early mining years and I had enormous sympathy with his point of view. I had to say, however, that being bitter against the Tories and supporting the Socialists irrespective of the change in conditions was not going to cure the terrible differentials in the human race. I was a Conservative, not because I was a politician but because I believed more in the principles of their policy than I did those of the Socialists. We would have some quite strong arguments on this score and I would end by saying, 'Johnny, what you say in theory is marvellous: I agree if it would happen this way I would support socialism one hundred per cent, but the plain fact of the matter is that people are people and they are good, bad and indifferent; and in some cases you will find sheer dregs of humanity in any political party whatever their political views.' In the end we begged to differ, but it did not alter my respect for Johnson; I thought that when he had seen more of the world he might change at least some of his more radical or idealistic views. I said to him, 'I'm going to have to send someone to take over South Marston factory. He will be resident down there but will still be part of the Castle Bromwich team; would you like the job?' He was speechless for a few seconds and then replied, 'Would I like the job? This is a chance in a million. I only hope I can measure up to the confidence and trust you have in me.'

Johnny certainly did that. Being level-headed and serious about his work he was always to be relied upon. He was also aware of his own limitations and experience and when in doubt upon a particular technical point would take the trouble to ask for advice. He flew correctly if not brilliantly and I gave him the fullest praise for pulling off his first successful forced-landing in a Mark 21 at Moreton-in-Marsh.

I was shocked and upset when, some months after he had become settled at South Marston, Stan Woodley rang me up to say that Johnson had been taken into the RAF hospital that morning with chest trouble. I went down to see him remembering the grim stories he used to tell me about his childhood days in the drab mining villages of the North and a wave of sadness swept over me as I thought of his struggle through life, his achievements and his success; and then for it all to be torn from his grasp through no fault of his own.

I could not put my thoughts into words and there was not much that I could really do to help. Johnny stayed for treatment at the hospital and was then sent away to a sanatorium.

THE PRODUCTION of the Lancaster brought an additional spate of visitors and as a result any flying display programme had to be extended somewhat. Generally it took the form of a Lancaster first, with myself as pilot. I would normally start with a few low-level dives over the airfield, pulling up into a semi-stalled loop turn, then a few low vertical turns with full power on all engines to cut off two engines on the port side and feather the airscrews as we went round, and then do a figure-eight on two engines in power and finish doing a vertical turn round the aerodrome turning with the engines on the top side. This seemed to impress the Americans more than anyone, as they were surprised a machine the size of a Lancaster could turn so steeply with the engines on the top of the turn. I never rolled the Lancaster on demonstration as I felt it seemed a little irresponsible and not in keeping with the purpose of the visit and also I needed plenty of room so as not to overstress the machine. As I landed, a flight of three Spitfires would take off for a session of formation flying; I would usually tell Olaf to lead, with Venda and one of the other better pilots to formate. When they had finished their show I would then take off in another Spitfire for the usual individual demonstration. Sometimes VIPs requested a flight in a Lancaster and this was done with every degree of decorum, unless it happened to be a visiting allied pilot's mission that wanted to see the whole works, when I would go through the normal test drill. Most visits were more friendly than formal and some showed a knowledge quite unexpected: the Duke of Kent showed unusually keen interest, but it was shortly after his visit to Castle Bromwich that he was killed in a Sunderland flying accident. Morganthau, Edward Stettinius, Mrs Eleanor

Roosevelt and some other American visitors I thought were more for a political motive than any moral or technical value. Mrs Roosevelt was humorous inasmuch as she was a bundle of vitality and rushed the entourage of press and security men off their feet. They got their own back when she sometimes inadvertently turned the wrong way in her hurry, by shouting en masse, 'No, not that way Eleanor.'

As 1943 drew to an end we all wondered what the new year would bring. Certainly we were getting prepared for the invasion of Europe, wherever it took place and when. The main road as I cycled from The Ridings to work was packed from end to end with hundreds and hundreds of tanks, and many other main roads were used in a similar manner. It was rumoured that we should commence the invasion from Scotland, with a landing in Norway, and I was told that the Lancasters when ready were to be delivered north to such places as Lossiemouth. This as we later learned was a feint to put off the enemy.

The weather was at its worst for an English Christmas and New Year: rain and more rain, no sun for weeks on end and the days dark with cloud. On 22 December in Spitfire MJ824, which I was flying for the first time, I felt the now accustomed piston thud at 3000 ft and then again at 7000 ft. This was so usual that I continued to climb after noting height and figures on my pad, but at 11,000 ft severe vibration set in suddenly and before I could close the throttle there was a terribly destructive noise from the engine followed by the usual plumes of oil and glycol smoke. I immediately switched off, but the windmilling airscrew continued to break things up still further in the engine. There were several layers of cloud and for once I could not see my old friend, the steam from Hams Hall. The last layer of cloud was fairly low and I was very tempted to bale out, but I reckoned I was either over Coventry or the south side of Birmingham. I knew if I didn't break cloud fairly close to either Elmdon or Castle Bromwich I was going to be in trouble and I wouldn't have time to do much about it. As I glided noisily with the engine shaking the airframe I thought I saw a column of white smoke over to the right just before I entered the last layer of cloud; if this was so then I reckoned it would be Hams Hall and that I was well over Birmingham. With nothing to lose I turned sharply right in the direction I had seen the steam and with my mouth very dry I hung on, tensely peering at the swirling cloud around me, praying I would at least be over open country when I was able to see. The first thing I saw as the machine broke cloud was the Fort Dunlop factory and ahead was Castle Bromwich airfield; in fact I was almost on it and had to lose what height I had in a very rapid and erratic fashion to get into the airfield at all. The Spitfire landed OK without damage, but if I had not seen Hams Hall steam for those split seconds and altered course when I did, I reckon I should have finished up somewhere in the middle of Birmingham city.

Although we had engine failures from time to time on the Wellingtons and Lancasters, at no time did I have to put one down in a field and all were luckily returned to base. On New Year's Eve of that year, however, I nearly had to force-land Lancaster DV279 for rather stupid reasons. Because of weather we were hard pushed for several weeks and there had been no breaks over Christmas. This was the first flight in this machine and Bill Buckley was my flight engineer. The machine seemed to be a good one and we had been about half-an-hour in cloud without a break, so I decided to do the dive and break cloud for a spot check on our position. It was raining hard and the light was not good. As we came out of the cloud I thought I saw a church and a factory, which I knew was to the north of Castle Bromwich; shouting to Bill we were OK I pulled up again to complete the tests. Unfortunately for me what I had seen was a church and a factory quite similar to the ones near Castle Bromwich, but which were in actual fact to the south of Birmingham and not to the north. Just then Bill shouted, 'Starboard outer oil pressure gone.' I replied automatically, 'Feather.' With one engine out I decided to return to Castle

Bromwich from the position I reckoned we were at that
moment and I headed sou'west. When we again broke out of
cloud to my surprise and consternation I did not recognise a
solitary thing and to make matters worse the rain and cloud
were now mingling with the low hills that seemed to have
appeared from nowhere. I was far from happy and could not
understand what had happened. Bill gave me another shock
when he shouted, 'Starboard inner pressure going.' This time
before telling him to feather I had a look at the pressure and
temperature myself, and then told him to feather as the glycol
gauge was going up alarmingly. I was now thinking very hard.
In a few moments I was going to have to put down in the best
field I could find as the rain came down harder and the cloud
got lower. The compass had not been swung but I had a pretty
good check all the time with the wind direction and we were
still travelling, albeit slowly, south-west. I glanced at the
altimeter and the high ground now too damned close for comfort and swung the machine round to head in the opposite
direction. I was certain I was way west of Birmingham; how,
I didn't know. I shouted to Bill, 'Sorry Bill, but I reckon we
are going to celebrate the New Year in a field, on our belly;
let's hope to God the port engines keep going.' The light was
beginning to go but I held on to the new course I had set and
we crawled along praying something would turn up. I was
angry with myself for being so careless and worried: Barbara
might have telephoned my office as it was New Year's Eve
and they might have told her I was overdue. Just when things
were looking very nasty indeed I saw something I recognised.
Immediately everything began to fall into place and I realised
what had happened. We landed on the two port engines at
Castle Bromwich and no one had even noticed that we were
longer than usual, except they were concerned about the light;
all the hangar lights were on as we swung onto the flight apron.

The year 1944 was one of hope and enormous expectancy
as rumours of a second front grew. On 27 January in LA187
I flew the first production Mark 21 from South Marston. It

was a dismal flight, disappointing for those on the ground: the constant-speed unit failed on take-off, the chassis would not operate properly and with South Marston airfield at the time in a rather poor state I decided to fly on to Castle Bromwich and hope I would land OK. This I did, but it was some days before we were able to fly the aircraft again.

When I had had my first opportunity of examining the latest addition to the Spitfire stable, my immediate reaction was that the genius passed on by R. J. Mitchell had died. The beautiful symmetry had gone; in its place stood a powerful, almost ugly, fighting machine. The classic lines had been replaced by forceful features and I had to push my emotions to one side and remind myself this was not a pretty toy, it was a fighting machine designed to enter a battle yet to be won and it would go into that battle with all the strength we could muster. Whatever my thoughts had been on the ground, I had cause to revise them in the air. Although the Rolls-Royce Griffon was similar in basic design and development it was of course a much larger engine; it had in fact 23 per cent greater swept volume than the Merlin. The installation allowed the nose to droop slightly, it was longer and in many ways it reminded me of a carnivorous pike in looks. This nose droop improved the pilot's view ahead but at the same time it necessitated a reduction in the airscrew diameter to 10 ft 5 in. in spite of larger oleo legs. The brake horse-power had gone up to 2400 hp, but the wonderful Merlin note was now missing.

The take-off was uncomfortable: the powerful torque needed a great deal of rudder to control it and the port wing dipped badly until the machine was well under way. (When we fitted the contra-rotating airscrew the take-off of course was completely changed for the better.) The moment the engine was started, I was very conscious of a much larger and heavier machine than the old Spitfire. In fact the weight had almost doubled since I first flew from Castle Bromwich. The climb after the take-off was quite startling and at first I thought my stop-watch was playing tricks when I reached 40,000 ft from the ground in just over 10 minutes. In level flight at 27,000 ft I found I was moving through the air at almost exactly 100 mph faster than I had done at Eastleigh in the early days of war and that I was doing it at about 10,000 ft higher. On the first tests we were advised by the design office to dive to 520 IAS, and at that speed you were certainly aware that you were going down. Later this diving speed was reduced to 500 IAS.

The most noticeable feature of the Mark 21 and 22 was the ailerons—if I remember correctly, piano-hinge attached throughout their length, mass-balanced within the wing structure and tab assisted on the trailing edge. I seem to remember Joe Smith discussing the mass-balancing; as lead was not heavy enough within the restricted movement due to the narrowness of the wing section he facetiously said, 'Well, we must use gold.' I do remember that the flight-rigging gave us a little trouble to start with. On the previous design the ailerons got progressively heavier with speed but they were, within reasonable margins, stable. On the Mark 21 the stability was not positive. The pilot could certainly put the aircraft into a horizontal level position and it would stay there, but if moved into a right- or left-hand turn the machine would not return to the level position unless assisted. The lightness of control, however, at very high speeds was such a tremendous improvement over the Mark IX and all other models that one revelled in aerobatics at speeds that would have been impossible before. I could now execute rolls and aileron turns at speeds of over 500 IAS with ease. With previous Marks not only would one not have been able to reach this speed but in approaching it the ailerons would have been almost rock solid and there wasn't enough room in the sky to get round. Nevertheless, at the low end of the speed scale the new type aileron did have certain shortcomings—in a very slow roll-over, say from the top of a half-loop, when on full power and with the machine well below the normal stalling speed, the ailerons became ineffective and came up against the travel stops, so that you could do nothing about it. Also it was much more difficult to induce a flick-roll and control the precise position when to stop it. As expected, I now needed more airspace in which to operate. Plummeting down vertically from 6000 ft or 7000 ft onto an aerodrome could now not be done within the confines of Castle Bromwich— I had to allow more room to pull out and I was also aware that my margin for pulling out of the dive had of course been reduced.

It was without doubt a great tribute to the team that Mitchell had left at the time of his tragic death. Had he been fortunate to have lived in this traumatic period of our history I fancy he might have shuddered at the lack of grace his creation had picked up, but at the same time I am sure he would have marvelled at the strength, the aggression, the agility and the speed that the little fledgeling had grown into. He would have been proud to have known that this little fighting machine started the war as one of the best in the world and at the end of nearly six hard years of bitter fighting in all parts of the globe it would remain so. He would also have taken pride in the fact that his dream achieved supremacy in three distinctly different theatres of war—as a fighter, at sea and as a photographic reconnaissance aircraft. I am sure he would have been astonished if he could have seen the few gallons of fuel originally installed in the Spitfire increased to 198 gallons, and what his thoughts would have been if he had known that eventually with external tanks the load was built up to 368 gallons is difficult to imagine. Despite all this, as far as is known the Spitfire only suffered about twenty-five structural failures in flight. I certainly never had one and never at any time did the airframe itself put me in any danger through design or structural weakness or fatigue.

The same thoughts can be applied to the Merlin and the Griffon, whose power output was increased enormously by continual improvements in design. With the introduction of the two-stage blower results were achieved that were inconceivable a short while before. I remember no failures that stemmed from design weaknesses. Inevitably the pressures of wartime demanded shortcuts in production, as with the piston failures. These in no way detract from the superb design and fantastic performance of these great engines.

The monthly check on full performance trials now necessitated a flight to 45,000 ft or over in the Spitfire and 29,000 ft in the Lancaster. The former was completed easily and quickly unless I had to check for stability due to change of a new type airscrew or some modification, but the Lancaster was more ponderous. Also for the first time I had to think of others as well as myself. This was brought home to me abruptly when once we were creeping up to around 28,000 ft: a member of the crew came forward and said, 'Eric Holden is either asleep or unconscious.' Not wishing to break off the trials, which were at a fairly conclusive stage, I shouted to Billy Buckley to check Eric out quickly and they found that he had trapped his oxygen line; when this was freed he recovered quickly enough. It made me realise the seriousness of having a crew who were not medically fit and who could pass out on me with probably more serious consequences. From then on I made sure everyone who wanted to fly was examined by the Works Doctor. It was inevitable that with so much flying I would be unable to insist on my own crew, whom I knew well, being with me on every flight that I made, and I only assumed that new members had been carefully briefed before take-off. This rather loose system almost cost me my life and made me realise as never before the importance of a well disciplined, knowledgeable and clear thinking team, reacting immediately to the calls made upon them by the pilot. On 17 March in Lancaster HK540 we had flown for approximately half-an-hour and had landed with a few minor snags. On the 18th the machine was flown once again and appeared to be all right; at 10,000 ft we commenced a power dive and had reached the speed of about 320 IAS when I heard a shout from my No. 3 to slow up; at the same time I felt a severe jolt go right through the machine, which then pitched into an uncontrollable dive, and in spite of every effort I could do nothing about it. We were in clear weather with a thick layer of stratus below at about 4–5000 ft. As I struggled to get the machine under control I heard my No. 3 shout something about the dinghy bursting out of the wing and striking the tailplane and wrapping itself round one of the fins. In seconds I was going to plummet into the cloud below, so noting my own chute was in place I gave the order to bale out to every crew member. To my astonishment as I hung onto the controls, ready to make my own desperate attempt to get out through the forward hatch, no one moved. The new flight engineer beside me stood petrified as if welded to the machine and although I screamed down the intercom the whole crew either could not or would not listen to me. For a split second I toyed with the idea of going it alone, but when I saw the look of fear on the man beside me I knew I could not leave him, and even if I had I doubted whether I could have got past him on my way down to the hatch and snapped my chute on in time before we hit the ground.

We were now in cloud with me almost standing on the instrument panel in my frenzied attempt to pull the machine out. It would not budge and the dive got progressively steeper and faster; I realised that within seconds of us breaking out of the cloud we should be making a very nasty hole somewhere around Birmingham. Just then I felt something give; I assumed later it was the dinghy tearing away from the tailplane, for the machine suddenly responded to the elevator control. We came out of the dive over the tops of houses on the north-east sector of Sutton Coldfield, with me in a bath of perspiration from my physical exertions at the controls and my frustration at not being able to get out of the aircraft or get my crew to make the first move. When we landed and the crew saw the extent of the damage to the tail, it was very easy to appreciate why I could not control the machine; my immediate relief was then rapidly displaced by cold anger as I began to realise I had nearly been killed by a crew who were either deaf or stupid and unfit to fly as a test team. I called them into my office later, when they had recovered from the shock, and told them in no mean

manner what I thought. Each man swore he did not hear my
instructions, but as I said at the time, 'You make bloody sure
you do next time, because if you think I am going to wait and
be killed because of a lot of stupid fools like you, you've got
another think coming. Next time you'll find yourselves on your
own.' I then told Buckley, Holden and Hastings to select
carefully those whom they thought would make a good flight
team and to send them to me for a very thorough briefing on
what to do in a similar emergency and in particular to ensure
that they knew how to test and use the intercom.

I suppose on average we had about the same ratio of engine
failures on the Lancasters as we did on the Spitfires, but
whereas it was often very dicey in the Spitfire, the Lancaster
was only subject to a passing comment in the air or on the
ground as we gazed into the gaping hole in the crankcase or
cowling.

I had another bearing failure and seizure when I flew
MK914 on 21 March, but a landing was made at Castle
Bromwich without further damage. Then, in June, the news
we had all been waiting for came: the Allies had landed in
Normandy. For months the most likely point of the Allied
landings had been debated between us. None underrated the
Germans and most had the greatest respect for their formidable
strength and disciplined organisation in war. We knew so well
that whilst the Channel had been our saviour in the past, it
could now be a devastating obstacle if things went against us.
The latest news that the weather was deteriorating hung over
everyone like a storm cloud as we listened to every scrap of
information we were able to glean. If the landing failed the
outlook would be grim indeed, for there were ugly rumours
that the enemy had new weapons on which he had concentrated development and they were about to be put into action
at any moment. When the breakthrough at Caen came, the
relief was intense and although most of us were confident, we
realised we still had a long way to go.

My own work over this period had changed somewhat. We

had now such enormous production, scattered over such a
wide area that with so many pilots testing I had my work cut
out to keep pace with organising our programme and checking
their reports, which would be frequently interrupted as a pilot
asked me to recheck for some unusual fault. We were still
having our crops of engine failures but now they were more
widespread as to the cause. I had another engine seizure in
Spitfire MK968 which Flight Lieutenant Ayerst had asked me
to fly because he thought it did not sound quite right. He was
one of the very young and inexperienced pilots who had not
been with us long, but what he lacked in aeronautical knowledge he made up for with his keenness and enthusiasm for the
job. And then on 19 October Flight Lieutenant Loweth landed
in Spitfire SM199 and reported that he had flown the machine
several times and would have cleared it but for the fact that at
the end of his full-throttle run, the engine had misfired for a
short period and then had cleared as he throttled back. Loweth
was another of the younger RAF pilots sent to us during this
period. He had the advantage of being a local boy and lived
only a few miles from Castle Bromwich. (If my memory serves
me correctly, he was the last pilot to leave our team and in fact
flew the very last Spitfire from the factory when I was some
thousands of miles away in South Africa.) I handed the
machine over to Alex Pitt, the Rolls-Royce representative, and
he suspected the plugs, as we had had a number of machines
recently with failures of a similar nature. I said I would give
the machine a thorough testing when Pitt had cleared it.

For some time I flew the machine in perfect weather and
thought it must be OK. I did a full-throttle climb to 18,000 ft
using both the MS and FS superchargers and all instruments
indicated a normal engine with average performance. I then
dropped down to 10,000 ft and did a full-throttle level run
with 18 lb boost and 3000 revs. I had hardly built up to full
speed when the engine suddenly surged violently; as I eased
the throttle back this ceased and the engine then began to
behave normally. I flew around for a while with all instruments

normal, turning over in my mind the possible causes of mis-
firing. I decided to do another full-throttle run and then
return to Castle Bromwich. The moment I opened the throttle
to 18 lb boost there was one violent engine surge and then an
explosion that blew half the engine cowling off. This was not a
normal failure as there was no glycol or oil fumes apparent
and I suspected supercharger failure. I could see Castle
Bromwich away to the north in the clear conditions and with
plenty of height in hand I was able to land without difficulty.
When we examined the engine the whole of the air intake and
bottom cowling had been blown away by the force of the
explosion: there was a gaping hole in the supercharger casing;
the impeller blades appeared to have disintegrated and the
throttle linkages had been torn away completely.

We were now knocking hell out of the Germans and for the
first time we were able to think seriously of the future. I was
anxious to leave the Midlands as soon as the war in Europe
ended. None of us knew what would happen when we had
only the Japs to fight, but it was thought that not only would
the theatre of operations change but the type of warfare as
well. I decided to buy a home on the East Coast as we loved
the sea and would take up residence in September of that year.
I would then make an application for a course on aircraft
carriers, so that I should be in a position to take up any new
posting to the Far East, should it materialise. We loved our
new home, which we re-named 'Briarwood' after the Vickers
house of the same name, in which Dick and Dorrie spent the
war years at Four Oaks. Our first guest was Venda, whom I
asked to join me at a local farmers' shoot to which I had been
invited when it was known I had returned to Lincolnshire.
This was certainly an eye-opener for Venda, who had not seen
this form of British sport before. The sight of all those large
sparkling cars was one thing; and then when he overheard
two farmers discussing how many thousand pounds one field of
potatoes had made, he said to me with astonishment all over
his face, 'Please explain, Alex. I don't understand. Here there

does not seem to be any rationing of petrol or food and the war does not even seem to exist.' I tried to explain what to Venda seemed incomprehensible.

When we flew back to Castle Bromwich Dick called me over to his office and said, 'I have some bad news for you, Alex,' and handed me a signal he had received from Air Marshal Sir Wilfred Freeman. I have forgotten the exact wording but it was along the lines: 'Owing to the leakage of secret information on technical matters it has been decided to withdraw all foreign pilots from top secret factories, this instruction to be carried out forthwith.' I was shattered and asked Dick if he could not do something about it. 'I have already tried, Alex,' he said, 'and there isn't a chance. It applies throughout the country.'

I of course had the miserable job of breaking the news to Snell, Ulstad and Jicha and I didn't relish the job. I called them into my office one at a time. What does one say to men who have fought for your country and with whom you have worked almost night and day for years, in conditions that weld a comradeship which is wellnigh unbreakable?

I spoke to Snell first of all: 'Ossie, the Managing Director has suggested that with the war progressing as it is I should send Allied pilots back to their own units.' Snell made my task so much easier when he butted in, 'Sure, I've been thinking the same thing. When we beat the krauts to their knees I'd like to be with my own mob as much as I have appreciated being here.' Ulstad was not so easily conned; he paused and the twinkle in his eyes told me that he knew more than he let on. 'Ja,' he answered, 'I understand what you have to do. When do you want me to go, Alex?'

Jicha was another kettle of fish. I found I couldn't lie to him. He went as white as a sheet and for a while he was speechless. Then he spat, 'I fight for our survival, I fight for the British when they are desperate; you are my friend and I trust you, but I hate the British.' I interrupted, 'Venda, hold on a minute, you are taking this too personally. I hate it as much as you do;

I think it is very shabby treatment; it leaves a dirty taste in my mouth, but let's be reasonable. We are only small cogs in a very important machine. Someone has tripped up somewhere but this is no reflection on you. I have tried to do what I can but the ruling is quite irrevocable. I have put you up for the AFC and I am assured it will be awarded without delay. You know what I think about you and after all the chances are you will be back in your own country before long.' Venda was not to be smoothed down, 'The Air Force Cross,' he spat. 'I don't want your baubles. I thought I knew the British better than this.' And with that he stormed out of my office, leaving me empty and ashamed.

It was a sad affair. After all those months of working closely together there was no celebration: the circumstances did not encourage it. Each man went as his posting came through. The parting was unhappy and uncomfortable and I waited dejectedly for the new influx of pilots to arrive.

SQUADRON LEADER PELLETIER was the first to
come, he was an Australian bomber pilot from Victoria,
with dark hair and complexion; quiet and unobtrusive in
manner, he was not a typical Australian. The next was Squadron
Leader Ellis, a competent pilot who had risen from the ranks
and who I now had to make my number one on Spitfires. All
this changeover meant a great deal of detailed briefing and
working the pilots into a job with which they were completely
unfamiliar. It had its amusing side, however.

I started with Squadron Leader Pelletier in a Lancaster,
and having gone through all the ground work and checks, we
took off. 'Check the wheels for balance before you stop them
with your brakes,' I said to Pelletier as we left the ground.
'Starboard wheel is badly out of balance; don't synchronise
your engines until you have reached rated altitude, but set
them very accurately at 2850 revs and full throttle which
should be 9 lb. Check with the Flight Engineer all the engine
pressures, temperatures, glycol temperatures with the radiators
closed and open; check all controls on the climb and note trim
tab positions.' We approached rated altitude, which with the
altimeter set at 1013·5 millibars and normal ambient temperature was at 12,500 ft. 'The outer starboard engine boost is
falling off too quickly, check the hot-air intake controls—yes,
they've crossed the controls; that one will have to be re-
assembled on the ground. Starboard inner seems to be OK, so
does port-outer; but your port-inner is down about ¾ lb;
either a leak in the boost line or rev counter wrongly calibrated
I would say.'

On this particular day the sky was completely covered by
thick stratus at about 3000 ft and as we broke through it into

brilliant sunshine we were able to carry on easily and un-impeded. We now checked essentials with a stopwatch and I continued: 'Drop your speed and then lower the under-carriage and check the time for lowering and raising; now the flaps, time up and time down with speed noted; now the bomb doors, check time and directional stability; now we check the stall, flaps up and then down; now level out at normal power and check all controls through the speed range and watch for aileron over-balancing; trim out carefully and mark trim tabs, also aileron position on the control column, which must be neutral when completed and may necessitate a change of wingtip or ailerons, depending on the tolerance.'

'We have enough snags now to return to Castle Bromwich,' I continued, 'but I will go through the whole drill as far as I'm able so that we can discuss details later. Now we should do a full-throttle level run, but as you have one boost down and a hot-air intake to change we'll do that on the next flight. We'll climb for the dive, which you should be able to do hands and feet off the controls as you set them on the trim tabs; next test rudders for directional stability, taking care not to overstall the fins; ailerons for smoothness of control and no over-balancing, and elevators for longitudinal stability and positiveness of control. At 360 IAS pull out gently after checking with the Flight Engineer the temperatures and pressures on all engines.'

We had now been up about an hour all the time in sunshine above the level layer of cloud. I said to Pelletier, 'Have you any idea where we are?' and he quickly replied, 'Haven't a clue.' I said, 'What would you say if we broke cloud right over Castle Bromwich?' He answered, 'I think it would be a bloody miracle.' Unbeknown to Pelletier as we had climbed out of the cloud I looked for my old friend Hams Hall steam, and below me directly on the portside I noticed a very slight disturbance to the otherwise level surface of the cloud, which I knew was the steam trying to break out to the surface. To the uninitiated there was nothing to see, but by long experience I had learnt better. During all the tests I had kept the little disturbed patch in the corner of my eye, using the sun as a datum point. I closed the throttle and swung the machine round into a steep turn as we entered the cloud and it was no surprise to me when the first dark patches of earth below showed up. I heard a gasp from Pelletier as he shouted, 'Well I'm damned! We are slap bang over the middle of the airfield.' The sequel to this was when Rosser saw me the next day and said, 'I don't know what you did to Pelletier but he told us at lunch today he didn't care what anyone said, but he knew you had something that we hadn't got.'

The war was not going well for us, Patton had broken through in a glorious rampage, Montgomery was having his arguments with the American generals, including Eisenhower, and at the moment we were held up at Arnhem.

I now travelled backwards and forwards to and from Strubby in Lincolnshire, which was a few cycling miles from my new home. Sandilands has now changed beyond recognition, like so many other charming places of our youth. As a boy, I thought it was the most tranquil and delightful spot on the whole of the East coast. A hamlet comprising less than a hundred well-built homes nestling against gloriously undulating sandhills and golden sea-washed beaches, it was unique. With the 18-hole golf course displaying those magnificently sited high tees way up in the dunes looking for miles out to sea or over the countryside and surrounded by rich open farmland heavily dotted with well-fed cattle, it created a pleasant border between the less attractive towns and villages on either side— as a young boy I felt I was entering another world. Most of the dwellings were occupied in the summer months by prosperous, well respected families from the Midlands. An atmosphere developed over the years which by today's standard might, perhaps, be considered dull, but at the time family after family would enjoy to the full the clean, healthy, active fun provided by sea, golf, tennis and riding. It was not unusual for a very elderly person to speak reminiscently of the days when there were no roads to Sandilands but only a sandy track from Sutton-on-Sea.

I would either use the Oxford or Dominie, or more often than not a Spitfire on test between the aerodromes. When our furniture had been removed after I had sold The Ridings, the last removal was my trustworthy cycle, which as it had belonged to my younger brother Eric, I was reluctant to part with. I had a Lancaster that day to climb to 29,000 ft, so I took the opportunity to take my bicycle in the aircraft over to Strubby. The weather at Castle Bromwich was quite good, but as I completed the climb and descended over the sea I was surprised to find very low cloud with heavy drizzle and poor visibility. There was quite a flap as we landed at Strubby, for all their machines were grounded, and the CO rushed up as he heard our engines overhead and wanted to know what was going on. We were not in radio contact so that when I appeared at the rear fuselage door to take down my bicycle from Bill Buckley, the Station Commander was literally speechless. When he had recovered he was kind enough to say he would find a safe place for my bicycle and as we had not stopped the engines of the Lancaster he said, 'All my chaps are grounded and if I had any authority I would refuse to let you take off.' I replied, 'Oh, it looks worse here than it is; at Castle Bromwich, where we are going, it's OK.'

I was on my way back from Strubby to Castle Bromwich in a Spitfire early one morning when the weather started to close in. It got so bad that I put down at Wymswold to check if the fog extended as far as the Midlands. I was conscious as I did so that something big was on: the aerodrome was crowded with American DC3s with gliders and hundreds of troops and supplies all over the place. As I stepped into the control tower the Commanding Officer, Group Captain Snaith, whom I knew, introduced me to the American officer in charge of the operation. He said, 'We've got to break through to Arnhem somehow; what's it like upstairs?' I said, 'Well, on the coast it's not too bad at ground level, but there are about three layers of cloud up to about 10,000 ft; and here as you know it's pretty grim.' We discussed the war for a while and then his second-in-command came up with the weather at Arnhem. The CO paused as he studied it, then he snapped, 'All stations go; we'll have a crack at it.'

As I took off for Castle Bromwich, a few minutes away for me, I pondered in admiration of those men who were about to embark upon an operation which in such weather alone was dangerous—but then to be shot at like sitting ducks as they attempted to land was worthy of praise beyond measure. During that period I was to see a frenzy of operations as the weather dealt a cruel blow to the operation. Unfortunately it was doomed to failure almost before it commenced, by a series of coincidences almost unbelievable, the worst of which was the German Panzer division regrouping in almost the exact position in which our troops were to land.

The weather did not help my own work now that I was living at Sandilands and many times I would fly over the customary fog at that time of the year, on a direct course until I picked up Hams Hall steam. Sometimes I could get into Castle Bromwich and at other times I would have to go all the way back to the coast. In the early days of the war it was rare indeed to see another aircraft above cloud and one could fly almost with impunity in and out of cloud anywhere at any time quite safely; now, however, it had become quite common to fly through heavy cloud on a climb and as one broke through into the sunshine it would be to find flight after flight of B-24s grouping for one of their heroic daylight raids over Germany. Also, if I went into Strubby at dusk or at night as I often did, I had to use the utmost care as the sky would literally be filled with Lancasters on their way to one of the 1000 bomber raids. Remembering the terror of being under heavy bombing raids earlier in the war we knew well what it must have been like to be on the receiving end of those attacks.

The tempo of our work did not ease; in fact I think there was even a more determined effort to bring the war to a successful conclusion as quickly as possible, before the Germans had a chance to do more harm. We got rid of the Lancasters from our own airfield as soon as they were completed and as a result I had a few Siberian-style trips over the Scottish Highlands to such places as Lossiemouth. On one such trip I saw Pelletier go ahead in one Lancaster and as I followed a few minutes later it was to run into cloud over the mountains. Guessing Pelletier would go round by the coast I dead-reckoned a course to Lossiemouth with a let-down over the Firth of Moray, and said with a grin to Bill Buckley, 'What's the betting we'll be there before Pelletier, Bill?' I regretted those lighthearted words soon afterwards, as the cloud turned out to be a real Arctic blizzard, and in no time at all we were so iced up that it was impossible to see a thing. The fine powdered snow was forcing its way into every little crevice; so that Bill and I shivered together as I worked out how much more ice and snow the Lancaster could take. We let down cautiously and with relief saw the Firth below and within sight of Lossiemouth. What we could see of our own machine looked as if we had just dropped from the Arctic itself. Bill stuck his thumb up as we circled the aerodrome, as Geoffrey Pelletier had not arrived, but the Rapide, which had been sent off well before to pick us both up, was on the tarmac waiting to take us back; so I knew that the weather around the coast was not too bad and that Pelletier would not be long.

I had some very sad news awaiting me when we returned. 'Hoots' Gibson telephoned me and said, 'You'll be sorry to hear, Alex, that Jicha has just been killed.' Apparently he had been posted to a maintenance unit in Scotland and was being flown from Kinloss in an Anson by an RAF squadron leader; they had crashed into the mountains, the squadron leader being killed outright. Venda, I was told, was comparatively unhurt; but as he attempted to crawl through the deep snow to safety, he passed out through exposure in the arctic conditions and the search party found his frozen body the next morning. A wave of intense sadness went through me as I was told. In spite of our different nationalities, the tremendous contrast in our upbringings, and the gap in many ways of our political views, I felt Venda and I understood one another without the use of words. I respected him and I made a promise to myself that when the war was over I would go to Czechoslovakia, find his mother and sister if they were alive and let them know what a magnificent job Venda had done throughout the war, and the affection and respect he had won from all those who had got to know him.

To this day I wrestle with my own conscience. When the time did become possible for me to visit Czechoslovakia the political climate over Europe had changed so dramatically I was afraid that any false move made on my part might set in motion a train of events embroiling the whole of Venda's family. When I had discussed such things as his feelings for Russia and communism, he had made it very clear that, although he had considerable sympathy for Russia as an ally and also as a Slav, his hatred for communism could not be contained. Remembering his attitude when Germany invaded his country, I am quite sure he would have been just as bitter later on, had he lived.

As one of the first to motor to Moscow when Russia lifted her iron curtain in 1957, I was aware of the close and careful scrutiny given to us as Barbara and I crossed the devastation in Germany, Poland and the towns of Minsk and Smolensk before running into the Russian capital itself. I realised then, that to find Venda's family would necessitate informing officials of my motives for wishing to see his mother and sister and the reason for our association over such a long period in the war. After careful thought I realised I could precipitate something very unwelcome if my language was misunderstood and I reluctantly decided to leave it for another day.

Our leave rota gave all the pilots generous weekly time off and there were also longer periods of leave monthly if it could be arranged. I did expect, however, for every pilot to be on his toes when he was on duty and if some thought I was an easy push-over, they soon had to think again. On one of our urgent trips to Scotland with the Lancasters, I arrived to receive a message that a pilot had returned because of weather; this was fair enough, as I would never tell a pilot to push on if he thought conditions were not good enough for him to do so. On landing back at Castle Bromwich in the Dominie, however, I was informed by Ellis that the pilot had landed at Leeds. 'What the hell did he want to do that for?' I exclaimed. Ellis replied with a grin, 'Well, he's off on a week's leave today and his wife is living in Leeds; so I guess he thought he would save himself a trip.' I said, 'Well, you get hold of him right away and tell him to finish his job before he has his leave.' Ellis replied, 'I've already been in touch with his address and he left there early this morning.' I wasn't very pleased, so I rang the Leeds police and after explaining who I was asked if they could trace a pilot who was wanted on an urgent mission and get him to telephone me as soon as possible. To my surprise they were able to locate him that day and he rang me asking what the flap was about. I said curtly, 'You've got a job to do, and your leave can start when you have completed it. I will send off a collection aircraft as soon as you advise us you are ready to leave.' The Lancaster was delivered the next day.

On 24 February the Managing Director telephoned me to say he had an important meeting at Weybridge: could I arrange for an aircraft to take him over in the afternoon? I was busy doing stability trials with metal ailerons at 45,000 ft in a Mark 21, so I told Rosser to stand by with the Dominie. I was in my office as they were about to take off, when a telephone message came through from Weybridge to say the weather had clamped down with heavy snow, reducing visibility to a hundred yards. I was very surprised as I had seen the outskirts of London from 45,000 ft and the conditions at that time were perfect. I ran out onto the tarmac and said, 'Weybridge have been on the phone to say the weather is hopeless; I think it would be better if you went by car.' Dick said, 'I can't make it by car now as the meeting is in an hour's time.' I said, 'I'll fly you as far as I can if you don't mind a rough trip.' Dick replied, 'I'm in your hands Alex; see what you can do.' I took over from Rosser and asked him to keep a sharp lookout from the passenger seat. The weather was so perfect that I thought Weybridge were having a big leg-pull, but then in the distance as the Chilterns showed up I could see a massive front descending on High Wycombe; the snow was falling so thickly that I could already see the distinct line on the ground where it had begun to settle. I checked my course, track and time carefully just as we penetrated into the snowstorm: if I could hold my course exactly I should intercept the railway line that went round the Brooklands track; if I missed it there was not much chance of my finding Weybridge. I was concerned at first by ice or snow build-up on the machine but was relieved to note that the snow was wet, hung for a while and then broke away from the wings. We could see nothing except directly below and then not a great deal. I knew that unless we picked up the railway line soon I should have to turn back, as there might easily be barrage balloons suspended over London and the outskirts. I spotted the railway line and clung to it like a leech. We came to a junction. At that point I knew Brooklands should lie, but although it was only yards away I was unable to see it. I edged over a little to the left and saw the hangars and the Brooklands clubhouse under my wheels; closing the throttle I swung round the area I knew so well and landed. As I taxied carefully forward I saw I was near the Vickers Flight Sheds. No one came out as we stepped out into the blinding snow and then as Rosser ran over to the office men appeared from everywhere and a car was soon on its way. Dick had not enjoyed the trip, but he was excited on two counts: one, that we had managed to get there by air; and secondly, that he was not late for his meeting. He tried to persuade me to stay, but I said I would go right away before too much snow had settled on the machine, the engines of which were still ticking over. Dick told me afterwards that it was laughable going into the boardroom: the Directors had already started the meeting

with apologies for Dick's absence, as they had been informed
by the pilots' office that the conditions were impossible. Dick
said he calmly opened up by saying, 'I thought the meeting
was for 4 o'clock, gentlemen. My watch says it's two minutes
to four. Perhaps it's slow.'

That particular weather front broke up a fine spell and for
a few days we had quite a build-up of machines. I had stayed
most of the week with our close friends at Streetly, the
Beauchamp-Brown's, but as we got the situation under control
I decided after a heavy day to do the last job on a Spitfire on
the way home as dusk fell. We had at that time a fine team of
pilots and the whole programme seemed to be going very
smoothly. I noticed as the flight reports came through, however,
that Flight Lieutenant Brew was getting in an unusually big
proportion of the tests; he had been with me some time and
was a fine, clean, good-looking type. When he first arrived he
smiled and his eyes lit up so much as we were introduced that
I said, 'Have we met before?' He replied, 'Not really, sir; but
I shall never forget the time I touched your Mew Gull at Speke,
during the Isle of Man races, when I played truant from school.
I never dreamt in my wildest dreams that I should be flying
with you on a job like this.' Examining the flight reports
carefully, I went to Brew on the tarmac and said, 'Jimmy, why
are you putting in so much more time than the other pilots?'
He coloured up and said, 'I was hoping you would not notice
it. I've only got a few hours to make up my first thousand, and
I was hoping to get them in before the end of the month. I've
spoken to the other chaps and they don't mind me hogging it
for a while if you don't.' I replied, 'No, it's OK by me, but
don't overdo it.'

I approached Strubby on this particular day just before the
Lancasters were due to take off on their first mission for the
night and the aerodrome was more or less clear to land. I knew
Flight Lieutenant Croft, the aerodrome control officer well,
and as I came to a standstill in the Spitfire, he ran over and
said, 'Vickers have been trying to get you on the phone.

Sounds terribly urgent, so I've got a call in for you now.' I ran up the control tower stairs, took the phone from a young WAAF officer and heard Eric Holden say, 'Flight Lieutenant Brew has just gone in with a Spitfire at Lindley. I thought you would want to know.' I paused and then said, 'I'm on my way back, Eric; have someone with an Aldis lamp ready, as I may have a job to see the airfield.' I turned to Flight Lieutenant Croft and said, 'I've got to get back in a hurry. Is it all right if I take off from the perimeter where I'm parked?' He nodded and I ran across to the Spitfire, snapped on my harness as the engine burst into life, and took off from where I was parked in a sharp climbing turn for Castle Bromwich.

The white steam from Hams Hall showed up clearly and I could see the dim outline of the sheds. As I turned, the bright light inside the hangar showed the doors were still open. I picked out the green Aldis lamp, which I knew would be at the east end of the runway. The Spitfire in those days had had the landing lights deleted, but it was no novelty for me landing by Aldis lamp and I waved a hand of thanks to the control officer as I taxied back to him after touching down. The grim news was soon forthcoming. Apparently Brew had gone in almost vertically from a great height right into the centre of Lindley aerodrome.* He had struck the soft ground with such force that although men had been digging since the accident occurred, they had not yet got down to his body. I went over to the scene with Dick, Reg Leech and Hoots Gibson, but as we discussed the accident with the Station Commander I was at a complete loss to understand it at all. I could not think that Brew had passed out in a normal flying position, as his harness would prevent him from falling onto the control column and the elevator trim tab position would prevent the machine from going into a very steep dive. He might have passed out whilst doing a power dive, but as this would most likely be at around 10,000 ft the possibility of loss of oxygen as the cause was I thought remote. The accident report suggested carbon-

* Today a Motor Institute Research Association testing track.

monoxide poisoning and they were sending parts of Brew's body to the laboratory in Birmingham for analysis.

Jimmy's death cast a gloom over all of us. I felt it deeper than I may have shown as I could not help thinking that if I had told him only to take his fair share of the flying, it would not have happened. The gloom was momentarily dispelled in a somewhat macabre manner, when the medical officer from Lindley telephoned me to say that specimens were on their way by air: could I arrange to have them handled carefully and delivered immediately to the University laboratory? When I told Stan, the stand-in ambulance driver, he was all eagerness and was there with the ambulance as the Lindley Wellington came to a standstill on the runway. We had not bargained for the parcel he was to collect, however. To his mortification the medical officer's assistant handed him an unwrapped large sweet-jar, filled with a clear solution, in which were floating, white and pink, some grisly remains of poor Jimmy. Stan took one look at the contents, went as white as a sheet and had to be brought back in the ambulance himself.

No carbon-monoxide poisoning was found and the cause of the accident remains a mystery. The report ended, however, by criticising the chief test pilot for not checking that every pilot under his control wore an oxygen mask for each test flight. I suspect this was a crack at me, as when questioned about our flight procedure I had stated without embellishments that although every pilot was briefed by me carefully, he was responsible for his own test procedure. My own people were indignant when I showed them the report: as they said, these were not novice pilots, but were picked for their ability and experience and would be the first to object and resent if they had a nursemaid for a CO. They expected me to demand a withdrawal of the criticism; but I was tired and depressed by the whole business and said, 'Forget it. I can't be bothered. There are more important things to do.'

After the initial shock and the failure of the Battle of the Bulge, the European war dragged on longer than expected and

I realised I had made my move into Lincolnshire a little prematurely; particularly as none of us knew what was going to happen when we had only to deal with the Japs. I found the journey back and forth a bit of a bind. I certainly raised the eyebrows of the local farmers, who knew me, as I cycled to Strubby early in the morning, wet or fine. Some would stop in their cars and offer a lift or even to give me petrol coupons; I said I had now been doing it for five years, so a little longer wouldn't hurt me, in any case I rather enjoyed the ride, particularly on a bright spring morning. As for the petrol coupons, I think they would have been a little surprised if I had told them that we probably consumed more in a day's work than they were likely to use for the rest of their lives.

The development work had intensified and I spent more time with Jeffrey at High Post, Worthy Down, Eastleigh or Hursley Park, particularly on the Seafire 45 fitted with the contra-rotating prop. We did a certain amount of work at Castle Bromwich, but it was more of a humdrum nature and less interesting; nevertheless it was on one of these humdrum exercises that I had my last forced landing in a Spitfire and almost my last flight of any kind in stupid but somewhat dramatic circumstances. For weeks we had been testing a Mark V with an empennage heavily loaded with lead weights to simulate landing and take-off loads that might be expected on the new prototype to be produced at Supermarines. No flying was involved, but only a simulated take-off down the runway to just below flying speed and then a close of throttle and a taxi back for another run. This went on and on until we were all heartily sick of it, particularly when the weights in the extremity of the fuselage were increased to such an extent that the machine became almost unmanageable when taxying, as the heavy tail would swing round suddenly rather like a heavy pendulum. We remedied this after one chassis had been written off, by controlling the tail wheel so that we could check the swing before it commenced. I offloaded a great deal of this work onto the other pilots and put Squadron Leader Ellis in charge of the programme. We had got up to 1500 lb of lead weights in the tail when Ellis came to me one morning and said, 'Would you have a go at this damned Mark V, Chief? I'm not very happy with it: the runway is not really long enough for a start, I can't get the tail off the ground; but I have the feeling the machine is about to become airborne.' I said, 'OK, Monty, I'll have a look at it as soon as I can fit it in.' I stepped into the machine without putting on my harness and the moment I started to taxi I realised the massive load we had in the rear. The runway we were using was really only our delivery road from the factory and knowing I could get another 200 to 250 yards alongside the Flight Sheds down to the Lancaster compass base, I told one of our police and flight inspectors to keep a check on the junction where the road met the flight apron, and I taxied down to get every available yard of run. I ran the engine up to maximum power and releasing the brakes the machine moved rather slowly forward with the tail of course hard on the ground for a hundred yards or so. It was just a very quick taxi, but then I began to sense what Ellis had feared. We were getting near flying-speed with the control column pushed hard forward but the tail was nowhere near lifting off. I held my hand hard on the throttle ready to snap it back if I felt we were likely to become airborne. I had practically made up my mind to discontinue the run when I came to the point where the Flight Sheds finished and the road began. There must have been a sudden gust of wind off the corner of the enormous building, as before I had time to do anything the aircraft suddenly shot up into the air at an incredible angle, in fact so near the vertical at about 40 to 50 ft up that my instantaneous reaction was that I must stop it flipping over onto its back and crushing me like a snail under a boot as it came down.

There was only one thing I could do and as I closed the throttle the tail touched the tarmac road, which flung the machine forward with such an almighty crunch that the machine virtually disintegrated: the chassis crumpled to nothing, both wings departed from the centre section, the engine came out of the frame, the fuselage was in half and petrol, oil and glycol spewed out flooding the road. To my complete astonishment and not a little relief, I stepped out unscratched. As I looked at the sorry mess I heard someone crying hysterically. Turning round I saw the young Works Inspector running towards me and sobbing his heart out. 'Oh, my God, oh, my God, I've never seen anything like it, I can't believe you're alive,' he blurted out. Even when I laughed and said I was unmarked he could not stop his sobbing and before the others arrived I took him gently by the shoulders and said, 'Now pull yourself together. No one is hurt and that heap over there is only an old Mark V; so what is there to get upset about?' 'Oh, Mr Henshaw,' he sobbed, 'I can't help it. I couldn't believe my own eyes when you shot into the sky.'

And then, suddenly, the war in Europe was over. I was tempted to take a Lancaster as we heard the news, loaded with our oldest Flight Shed team and do a tour of the bombed and battle-scarred areas of Germany. A day in good weather over the land which had caused so much stress in the world would not be to gloat, but to see history and to appreciate what had to happen to bring such an enemy to his knees. I gave up the idea, however, when I realised I could only carry a very small section of our now large team; this was bound to cause disappointment amongst those who were forced to stay behind. Dick rang through the next day to say that he, Reg Leech and myself had been invited to make a tour of the battle zones and we were to arrange with the RAF medical officer to have all the various inoculations required for such a visit. It was decided that the three of us should go in the Airspeed Oxford and would leave as soon as our uniforms were ready. Unfortunately Dick had to postpone several times due to his increasing commitments at Weybridge and in the end it was called off.

Now that the European war was behind us I began to think

out what form my activities would take against a naval power
such as the Japanese. I assumed that production would be
modified in our own country and that we might well be posted
somewhere convenient and accessible to the operations taking
place in the Pacific theatre. In any case it was quite obvious
that as we should be concerned with naval warfare my work
would be on fighters and bombers operating from carriers. I
soon found other pilots had been thinking on similar lines to
myself, for when I arranged for my course with the Fleet Air
Arm it was to be told that Harald Penrose, chief test pilot of
Westlands, and Geoffrey de Havilland with two other pilots
from Supermarines, would be there at the same time. As we
first of all had to fly to East Haven in Scotland, and I would
in any case use the Dominie, I invited the others to join me at
Castle Bromwich and we would all go up together. They all
arrived with the exception of Geoffrey de Havilland, who had
to cancel out.

The weather was wet and cloudy and because of the hills
en route we put a call in to East Haven to find out what it was
like there. They gave five tenths cloud with two miles visibility,
so we took off and climbed out of the dull mist and rain into
sunshine. My passengers seemed happy enough so I kept above
the cloud on a steady course with the intention if we did not
see the ground when my ETA was due of bearing a little east
and coming down over the sea. It was a pleasant flight, however,
as when we had passed over the Cheviots we saw patches of
green and brown below and soon were clipping over the water,
with the gulls and puffins diving as we passed Dundee on our
way into East Haven Naval Station.

I have always loved the Navy and the Fleet Air Arm and
everything seemed very shipshape when we were handed our
gear and shown to our spotless quarters by a trim, efficient-
looking Wren officer. We were each allocated a Fairey Firefly
for the check-out and carrier deck landings. I would rather
have had a Seafire of course, but the Firefly was a nice enough
docile machine. We were cleared for dummy deck landings

without trouble, and were pleased to see our rating on the control officer's report was above average.

Harald Penrose nearly had trouble once as his engine cut on take-off; fortunately he was not airborne and was able to pull up in time. When he told me that his engine had just faded on power but ticked over perfectly I was able to say with a fair degree of confidence because of my Spitfire experiences that I was sure it was a faulty boost control unit and explained to him how this could happen. We then flew over to Ayr when the East Haven Commanding Officer thought we were ready for the carrier landings, so that we could complete the course before going to sea, by using radio and code. The next day was bright and fresh and we set off in loose formation to intercept the *Premier*, an American escort-type aircraft carrier, somewhere off the Isle of Aran. I think we all spotted it at about the same time; I don't know what the others thought, but to me it looked about as big as a postage stamp. We went into line astern and awaited instructions from the aircraft carrier. I felt that most of the credit for the first landing should have been given to the control batman. I concentrated on him and only when my wheels actually touched and the landing cable drew me to an abrupt halt, was I conscious of the enormous superstructure, the long clean deck and the white tops of the thrashing waves with the seagulls trailing in our wake. Three of us landed, but the fourth, Harald Penrose, was flagged off on the third attempt and told to return to base. Apparently for some reason that he could not explain, he would persist in attempting to land on the carrier with a considerable amount of drift, and the batman waved him off as unsafe. He did some more dummy runs at Ayr and returned to the *Premier*, where this time he landed OK.

I thought the life on board an aircraft carrier at sea was marvellous. If the job of finishing off the Japs was to include more of this then it was going to be a pleasant change from Castle Bromwich. I think we were all sorry to leave.

But in a few short weeks the picture changed totally. I was

at home one weekend with Barbara and Alex fixing a light shade in the breakfast room, when Dad rushed in and said, 'The Americans have dropped an atomic bomb on Japan.' For a while we did not appreciate the significance, but then as the news filtered through we knew that this was the end of Churchill's 'blood, sweat and tears' spilt and spent over so many long, tiring and frightening years. The transition from war to peace had begun.

THERE was a subdued atmosphere, both in the factory and on the airfield. The spontaneous jubilation of VE and VJ days had long since died away. This feeling was accentuated by the diminution of staff and employees at Castle Bromwich; those that were left for the final clearance hung around bored and listless, no doubt brooding on what the future held in store for them. I would have liked in so many ways to have flown the last Spitfire to be produced in the factory, but the pace was now so slow and the days would have seemed endless watching solitary figures where thousands had been before. In any case I preferred to remember a vigorous giant working at full speed rather than the inevitable death of what seemed to be a sick friend. I decided I must make a move and accepted an offer to work with a company formed between Miles Aircraft Ltd and General Mining and Finance Corporation in South Africa. I had sold my last Tomtit to Supermarines and handed in all my keys; I was left with only my old black sheepskin boots, a fur flying jacket and a wall map of the world, which I had stared at so often in my office.

In January 1946 the day came for my last flight in a Spitfire, contra-rotating Mark 22, LA449. I climbed into the cockpit with the casualness of very long habit—no words were spoken— just a glance and the chocks moved away and the Griffon roared into life. As I climbed steeply from the airfield I reflected back over the years to my first flight from Castle Bromwich in a Mark II. I wondered if there had ever been a closer attachment and understanding between man and machine than had developed in the constant and often demanding association that had been my life for six years and four months. The Spitfire over those years had grown up and matured: its vigour and aggression had increased—I had grown older. Today the enthusiasm was missing. I sat, as on a well-trained horse whose movements were smooth and responsive; there was never any doubt that it would do as I wished or fear that I would ask it to do something beyond its capabilities.

My mind went further back to the summer of 1939, just before our carefree world collapsed. I was schooling a spirited iron-grey gelding called Quicksilver. As I nuzzled and blew gently into his nostrils, there was a soft snort of enjoyment; as we stared at one another I sensed we were taking stock—weighing up and deciding the calibre one against the other. We were both young, and the vigour and vitality bubbled over as we galloped the green fields that morning; the hooves pounding on the soft turf sent up a fragrance that lived with me so many times during those drab and dreary days of war. Intuitively we were testing each other and it took time to work up mutual respect: there were qualities and weaknesses, perhaps, on both sides. Quicksilver had been born in hard hunting country, could leap from double-bank to double-bank and was as agile as a cat. With the exuberance of youth we rushed at the complexity of fences, dykes, hedges and waterjumps, and at times we achieved a harmony of thought and action that was satisfying in the extreme. That experience taught me clearly that whatever happened only I could be in command, and that neither of us should attempt anything beyond our capabilities. I kept this lesson in mind when flying.

I thought of the summer evening in 1940 when so little had been produced and so much was expected from the works that now lay below me. It all seemed a lifetime ago, so much had happened since. We had kept our morale, we had produced our weapons and finally we had won our battles.

As I reached rated altitude on the second blower I levelled out and looked below at the vast sprawling mass of belching chimney-stacks. They had done much to bring us victory during those years of strain, hard work and tension. Away to the north-west the dull black smog spread so that I could scarcely see the spot at Willenhall where I had nearly left my bones in 1943. And then as I looked south-east I saw Hams Hall towers, the only thing in all that gloom I could call my friend—the steam pluming up in the still air so that it stood sentinel against the dark skyline.

I found I was doing the test routine automatically and as I jotted down the figures on my knee-pad I did so without interest. I thought of my future and my home and family. Quicksilver would by now have been older than me in horse years: if I were sitting his saddle now we would not be plunging into action with such gay abandon but moving more sedately and conscious of each other's mood. But I would never sit on Quicksilver's back again—like so many that I had held dear he had not survived the war.

I went through the final dive but allowed the machine barely to touch 520 IAS—I saw no point in overdoing things. It had just dawned on me that the war was over. I was free once again and in days would be leaving for a new life in South Africa. I should have been elated but instead I was cautious, withdrawn and inwardly depressed. I tried hard to analyse my feelings.

I think I may have sensed the future with some foreboding. At the moment of victory and triumph the British people had thrown out the man who had led the free world to safety. Churchill had always been my hero and I had not at any time seen another politician or statesman who had the foresight, the courage, the tenacity and such a feel for the will of the people. At a time when we were at our lowest ebb, when the rest of the world expected us to fall beneath the tramp of Nazi boots it was Churchill who roused our nation with a clarion call and put heart into those suffering the tyranny of suppression, torture, hunger and fear. Churchill had, in our most critical period of history, stood out a man above all others. And he had been rejected.

But as I thought of the weapons by which he had forged his way my heart lifted. It is, I suppose, rare to have one weapon that stands supreme or can contribute on its own to final victory in any war. There have of course been some near examples in our own time: the tank in 1916, the submarine in World Wars I and II and—the most extreme demonstration—the atom bomb in 1945. But I could with little effort state a case for the Spitfire winning the last world war. At the same time that it sustained and encouraged every man, woman and child in this small island of ours, it struck not only a physical blow but a strange psychological terror in the heart of the enemy—particularly in German pilots when out of the blue flashed that elliptical wing of perfect symmetry to spurt death and destruction that survivors would remember for the rest of their lives. In spite of the numerical superiority of the Hurricane and the excellence of its performance in battle, it could not have survived alone. Neither could we, had we lost the Battle of Britain. Whatever future historians may write and say, without the Spitfire we could not have survived the largest and most bitter contest for supreme power that has yet been known in the history of the world.

My last landing was a careful, gentle touchdown, and I taxied back to the Flight Shed as I had done so many hundreds of times before. The stillness around me seemed strange and unreal—where were my comrades of those six long years, the loyal and willing team who had always bustled around me when I came to a standstill, the highly skilled, courageous band of pilots? A few minutes later as I drove away, leaving that lone Spitfire on the vast, empty expanse of tarmac, I sent up a short prayer of thanks for being so closely associated with this classic of our time.

✳ *Epilogue*

SOME YEARS AGO I was invited by the Birmingham City Council to unveil a memorial on what had once been Castle Bromwich Airfield. Now, however, it had the more dignified title, Castle Vale. Instead of aircraft it now accommodated houses and apartments. I was to drive to Castle Vale, meet the Lord Mayor and other dignitaries, complete the ceremony, inspect the guard of honour and then be conveyed by helicopter into the City of Birmingham for lunch. As I approached along the winding road after leaving Tamworth, I saw the clouds of steam billowing up in the distance from the Hams Hall power station. It looked unchanged, a silent but significant sentinel which, to me, stirred the memories of bygone years. My route took me past modern Castle Vale—an unlovely forest of high and low rise dwellings. At first my reaction was to regret that I had agreed to come but I reminded myself that it was primarily for the pilots who had operated with me at Castle Bromwich during the period 1940–1946. Then I saw the old Spitfire and Lancaster factory production blocks—enormous, drab and dirty—but as busy as ever. This time churning out utensils of peace and not weapons of war.

During the colourful, noisy but sometimes moving ceremony that followed, I looked into the crowd and at the many faces which in some instances seemed vaguely familiar and the thought struck me that this was really an epitaph to the ordinary people. True, the pilots I had with me during those fateful years did an exceptional job—bank-clerk, architect, lawyer, artist, gunsmith, teacher, mechanic, undergraduate. They had been taught and trained well and had achieved greater than average skills as pilots before they were posted to Castle Bromwich. Their job with me was certainly taxing, sometimes dangerous, often frightening. They got back to comfortable quarters each night, they had adequate leave to compensate for my rigorous demands, they had the status of officers in uniform, and the prospect of promotion or a military award. If they were killed testing, it was done on 'active service' and their funeral would have the pathos of a military turn-out complete with Union Jack. Not so the ordinary people. They were caught up in the whirlwind of a world fighting for survival, suffering untold miseries as they carried on in a truly heroic manner. They coped with monotony, severe rationing, bombing at home and at work, continual worry over loved ones far away. Yet there they were, night and day, working like beavers under artificial light and in a noise level that gave me a headache: amidst the hiss of air lines, the rattle of rivet-guns and the crescendo of noise from powerful engines these unsung men and women strove, pushed, pulled and lifted to get the Spitfires into the firing line.

I thought of them then and I remember them now as a great people, the British race at its best. Amidst the drabness, the danger and the depression there was always the wonderful humour that rose like a ray of sunshine, often when you least expected it—subtle, raucous, frequently bawdy. Some, I know, are dead. Most have sunk into anonymity. But they have their memories of a most crucial period in our history of which they were a vital part. Their achievement can never be erased.

❈ Summary of flying from Castle Bromwich Works from June 1940 to January 1946

During this period 11,694 Spitfire aircraft and 305 Lancaster bombers were produced at Castle Bromwich and the dispersal factories of Cosford and Desford.

In the course of the production and performance trials completed on these aircraft, 8210 hours were flown on Spitfire aircraft and 344 hours on Lancasters, involving 900 Lancaster test flights and 33,918 for Spitfires.

During five years of flying, 25 pilots were engaged for six months or longer, the majority of these comprising RAF officers who had completed various tours of active service.

127 forced landings were made, largely due to engine failures of one sort or another. Out of this number, in spite of often appalling weather and the critical nature of the failure, 76 aircraft were landed with wheels down and no further damage.

Two pilots were killed during the course of these flights for reasons so far unknown.

One parachute descent was made with torn canopy after engine failure over fog. Five pilots sustained personal injuries.

In addition to the activities at Castle Bromwich, Cosford and Desford, the flight section of this factory was responsible at one period of the war for the flight testing of 71 Wellingtons at the Brooklands Repair Organisation at the Flight Sheds, Castle Bromwich; 180 Wellingtons at the Brooklands Repair Organisation at Sywell; 256 Spitfires and Seafires at Vickers-Armstrongs, South Marston; 1 Wellington at Vickers-Armstrongs, Blackpool; and 260 Spitfires at No. 1 CRU, Cowley.

The grand total of this work during the period that the flying establishment was maintained at Castle Bromwich amounted to:

12,767 aircraft flown
37,023 test-flights
9,116 hours and 10 minutes

This does not include communications flying with the Dominie, Tomtit, Gull and Oxford which were used during this period.

✳ Index

accidents, 2, 31, 33, 58–9, 71–4, 81–2, 88, 119–21, 125–8, 149–52, 174–6, 191–2, 194–5
aerobatics, 33, 39–42, 50–2, 53–5, 90–1, 122, 164
ailerons, 43–4, 78, 172
Air Inspection Directorate, 59–61
Air Ministry, 12
Air Transport Auxiliary, 67
aircraft carriers, course on, 178, 196–8
Aircraft Production, Ministry of, 34
airfields:
  Baginton, 115
  Boscombe Down, 111, 138
  Castle Bromwich, *see separate entry*
  Chester, 31
  Cosford, 57, 73, 95, 123
  Cowley, 37, 45, 47, 57, 73, 85, 114, 163
  Derby, 6
  Desford, 57, 73, 124
  East Haven, 196–7
  Eastleigh, 22–3, 30, 33, 73
  Elmdon, 6
  Hawarden OTU, 53, 55, 87
  Heston, 34–5, 147–8
  Llanbedr, 132
  Portrush, 86
  South Marston, 164–5
  Strubby, 183, 184, 185, 193
  Sywell, 47, 57, 58, 73
  Weybridge (Brooklands), 15, 16, 188–90
  Worthy Down, 73, 146, 158–9
airscrews, 77–9, 131, 133, 142, 146–7, 161, 168
appendicitis, 97–8, 160
Ashton, S/Ldr Tom, 122
Atcherley, David, 58
Austin Motor Company, 89, 90
Avro Works, 144
awards, 162
Ayerst, F/Lt, 177

bad weather flying, 26–7, 46–7, 100, 102–3, 160, 184–5
baling out, *see* parachute landings
Bancroft, Tommy, 47, 59

Bartley, S/Ldr Tony, 160
beam-landing, 160–1
Beaverbrook, Lord, 46, 47, 87
Becker, W/Cdr Bernard, 71, 73, 87, 109, 121, 131–2, 133, 155
Bird, Commander Sir James, 30
Birmingham Spitfire Fund, 51–2
black-outs, 139, 191
Blitz, 47–8, 62–3, 68–9, 104, 117
Boulton, Paul, 132
Brew, F/Lt Jimmy, 190–2
'Briarwood', 178
Bristol radial engines, 15
Brown, Sam, 144
Buckley, Bill, 72, 128–9, 169–70, 174, 176, 184, 186
buggy-cart for Alex, 163

Cape record 1939, 1, 3, 6
Carter, Amos, 141–2
Castle Bromwich,
  administrative difficulties, 63–7, 104, 155–6
  bombing of, 68–9
  Chief Pilot, 46–9, 73, 76–7, 94, 176–7, 192
  factory defence, 58, 86–8
  memorial to, 203–4
  Pig Club, 105–7
  pilots, 93–7, 98, 107–11, 154, 179–80, 190, 203–4, 205
  Spitfires, testing of repairs, 37–9
  statistics, 205–6
Chandler's Ford, 31–2, 35
Chateaubrun, Guy, Comte de, 4–5
Chrystall, Dr, 146
Churchill, Lady (Clementine), 69–70, 90, 92
Churchill, Sir Winston, 11, 89–93, 198, 201
cloud, flying in, 100–3, 163–4, 168–9
Clouston, Flying Officer A. E., 6, 9
Cobb, John, 16
Cook, Bernard, 38, 129–30
Cook, Miss, 108, 115
Cotton, Sidney, 18–19, 20–1, 34–5
Courtney, Bill, 6
Cripps, Sir Stafford, 146

Croft, F/Lt Bernard, 190–1
Cross, Jack, 4–5
Cullum, George, Gen. Man., Cowley Works, 45, 85–6
Cunningham, G/Capt John (Catseyes), 58
Curtis, Lettice, 67

Dancy, Wilfred, 12–13
de Havillands, 45
de Havilland, Geoffrey, 147, 148, 196
demonstrations, 42–3, 50–2, 53–5, 79–81, 90–3, 114–15, 140, 147–8, 167–8
Deterding, Henry, 22
Detroyet mission, 50
development flying, *see* research and development
Dickson, B. W. A. ('Dick'), 66, 71, 79–80, 88, 93, 104, 108, 121, 128, 132–3, 140, 141, 156, 160, 178, 188–90, 191, 195
Dickson, Dorrie, 71, 121, 141, 160, 178
displays, *see* demonstrations
Dodds, Chief Mechanic, 48–9
Donaldson, W/Cdr, 55
Dudley, Lord, 52, 90, 91, 116
Dunbar, Sir Alex, 38, 39, 43, 46, 47, 51, 53, 61, 63
Duncan, B. A., 16–18, 20
Dutch Royal Family, evacuation of, 45

Edwards, George, 20
Elliott, Joe, 77
Ellis, S/Ldr Monty, 181, 188, 193–4
Embry, Air Marshal Sir Basil, 58
Empire Test Pilots' School, 111
enemy aircraft, scares, 44–5, 56
Essex Aero, 4
Everett, Bob, 22
exhibitions, *see* demonstrations

fatigue, 138, 139
Ferry Pilot, film, 148
Field, Brian, 81–3
Firefly, Fairey, 196
fire-watching, 129–30
Fleet Air Arm, 33–4, 159, 196
Frankfurt International Air meeting, 1939, 6–9
Freeman, Air Marshal Sir Wilfred, 179

Gammon, Tommy, 18
Gardner, Lt/Cdr Jommy, 22
General Mining and Finance Corporation, 199
Gerbrecht, Herr, 6–7, 8, 11

Gibson, W/Cdr 'Hoots', 160–1, 186, 191
Gleeve, Sid, 144
Grierson, John, 114
Griffon engines, *see* Rolls-Royce
Guthrie, Giles, 22

Halifax, Lord, 140
Hampton-in-Arden, 'The Ridings', 6, 52, 55–6, 62–3, 84, 156, 184
Hams Hall power station, 100, 101, 149, 151, 168–9, 182, 185, 191, 201, 203
Handasyde, Bob, 31
Hare, Maurice, 15, 16
Hastings, Jim, 72, 94, 101–2, 104, 106, 176
Henshaw, A. ('Dad'), 4, 6–7, 11, 12, 13, 14, 20–1, 30, 57, 198
Henshaw, Alex (Jun.), 146, 150, 156, 162–3
Henshaw, Barbara, 4–5, 10–11, 12, 13, 14, 20, 29, 30, 32, 37, 38, 46, 47, 52, 56, 117, 119, 120, 121, 128, 145–6, 150, 162
Henshaw, Eric, 59, 184
Henshaw, Leslie, 70, 118–19
Hives, Lord, 130
Holden, Eric, 60, 72, 73, 82, 94, 95, 102, 129, 137, 162, 174, 176, 191
Home Guard, *see* Local Defence Volunteers
Humble, Bill, 147
Huntley, F/Lt Geoffrey, 98, 109
Hurricane, Hawker, 45, 89, 90
Hursley Park, 73, 76, 158

Immelmann, Max, 7–9
invasion scares, 57
inverted flying, 64–5

Jicha, Venda, 96–7, 98, 99, 100, 101, 102–3, 108, 112, 113, 122, 137, 154, 156–8, 167, 178–80, 186–7
Johnson, F/Lt Johnny, 98, 164–6

Kellett, W/Cdr Richard, 64–5, 70
Kent, Prince George, Duke of, 121–2, 167
Kerr, Deborah, 160
Kilner, Maj. Sir Hew, 46, 63–5, 70
King's Cup Air Race 1938, 1, 83

Lamb, F/Lt, 98
Lamplugh, Capt., 121
Lancaster, Avro, 132–3, 144, 149, 152–4, 157–8, 160, 167, 176

landings, forced, 48, 59, 70–1, 123–35, 137, 146–7, 169–70, 193, 205
Leech, Reginald, 105, 156, 191, 195
Levy, Len, 27, 31, 48
Local Defence Volunteers, 37, 38, 43
Lowdell, W/Cdr George, 93, 98, 100, 101, 122, 153, 160
Lowe, F/Lt, 98
Loweth, F/Lt, 177

Maintenance Unit pilots, 109–11
Marlborough, John Spencer Churchill, 10th Duke of, 116
marriage, 30, 32
mechanics, 48
Merlin engines, *see* Rolls-Royce
Messerschmitt 109, 9, 30
Miles Aircraft Company, 81, 83, 199
Mitchell, R. J., 30, 135, 136, 171, 173
Modley, S/Ldr Bill, 56, 57, 122
Mohne and Eider dams, 144
Morganthau, Henry, 167
Morris Motors, 37, 47
Munro, Mr, 85

Nelson, Arthur, 23, 25, 30

Olivier, Laurence, 22
Operational Training Units, 53–5, 87
O'Rourke, A. H., plate 38

Page, Bats, 58
Palmer, Horace, plate 38
parachute landings, 150–2, 205
Pelletier, S/Ldr Geoffrey, 181–3, 186
Penrose, Harald, 196, 197
Percival: Gull, 57, 58, 63, 75; Mew Gull, 1, 4, 6, 23, 25; Vega Gull, 5, 6, 8
Phillips, F/Lt, 147
phoney war, 35–6
Photographic Reconnaissance Unit, 35
Pickering, George, 21, 22, 26, 27, 28, 29, 31, 44, 46, 73–4
Pierson, Rex, 20, 135
Pitt, Alex, 177

Quill, Lt/Cdr Jeffrey, 14, 20–1, 23, 26–7, 29, 30, 31, 32, 33, 34–6, 44, 46, 48–9, 58, 73, 75, 115, 136, 140, 147, 158, 159–60, 193
Quill, Pat, 35

research and development, 46, 58, 139–40, 146, 158
Reynell, Dick, 45–6, 114
Richardson, Ralph, 22
'Ridings, The', *see* Hampton-in-Arden

Robertson, Lt/Cdr Don, 160
Robson, Guy, 22
roll manoeuvres, 41–2, 157–8
Rolls-Royce engines, 1, 33, 48
  Griffon engines, 171, 173–4
  Merlin engines, 1–2, 66, 130, 147, 173
    III, 25, 136
    XII, 44
    '45', 76
    '50M', 76
    '61' and '66', 135–6
Roosevelt, Eleanor, 168
Rose, Tommy, 18
Rosser, F/Lt Jim, 98, 112, 113, 154, 183, 188–9
Rugeley, 151

sabotage, 72
Sanders, F/Lt Sandy, 71, 73
Sandilands, 183–4, 185
Scales, E. R., 38
Sea Otter, 20, 26
Seafires, 193
seaplanes, flying of, 27–9
Seidemann, Major Ernest, 8, 11
Shepherd, Lt Jack, 79, 122
skewgear failures, 123–35, 142–3
Smith, Joe, 30, 172
Snaith, Gp/Capt., 184–5
Snarey, George, 57, 60, 67, 93
Snell, Ossy, 95, 98, 154, 179
South Africa, 199, 201
Spitfires,
  controls, 43–4
  de-icing trials, 27
  first flight in, 23–6
  last flight, 199–202
  losses, 53
  Mark I, 25, 50, 76
  Mark II, 39, 43–4, 91, 136
  Mark III, 44, 50
  Mark V, 75–6, 193–4
  Mark VIII, 136
  Mark IX, 135, 136, 146, 161, 172
  Mark 21 and 22, 146, 170–3
  repaired, 37
  vibration, 112–14
Stettinius, Edward, 167
Streetly, 47
stress, 83–4
Summers, Capt. Mutt, 13–15, 16, 20, 21, 30–1, 47, 135
Supermarines, 13, 21, 30, 44, 77, 158

Talamo, E. R., 38, 43, 61, 67, 141
'Ten in June, The', 47
Thomas, Sir Miles, 114
Thompson, W/Cdr Tommy, 57–8, 64
Thorne, Bill, 144

Tiger Moth, D.H., 45, 58
Tomtit, Hawker, 75, 86, 117, 119–21
towbars, 65–6

Ulstad, Olaf, 98–100, 107, 124, 154, 167, 179

Verney, Air Com. R. H., 38
Vickers-Armstrong Ltd, 13–21, 22, 31, 46, 153, 188–90
visitors, distinguished, 50–2, 69–70, 88–93, 121–2, 140, 167–8

Wallis, Barnes, 144
Walrus, Supermarine, 20, 26, 27–9, 35–6, 50

Waters, Dr, 120
weather, *see* bad weather flying
Webster, Gp/Capt., 13
Wellingtons, 15, 19–20, 31, 47, 146, 149
Wenman, Barbara, *see* Henshaw, Barbara
Westbrook, Trevor, 13–14, 16, 21
Whittome, Ken, 22
Wickham, Mr, 38, 61
Wilson, F/Lt L. D., 67, 71
Wood, Sir Kingsley, 18–19, 104
Woodley, Stan, 165
Woolston, 27, 30, 35, 50
World War II, outbreak of, 10–11
end of, 195–6, 198, 199

Bestselling War Fiction and Non-Fiction

☐ Bat 21	William C Anderson	£2.50
☐ Royal Navy and the Falklands War	David Brown	£8.99
☐ The Cocaine Wars	Paul Eddy	£3.99
☐ China Seas	John Harris	£3.99
☐ Passage to Mutiny	Alexander Kent	£3.50
☐ Colours Aloft	Alexander Kent	£2.99
☐ The Hour of the Lily	John Kruse	£3.50
☐ The Bombers	Norman Longmate	£4.99
☐ Convoy	Dudley Pope	£3.50
☐ Winged Escort	Douglas Reeman	£2.99
☐ Typhoon Pilot	Desmond Scott	£2.99
☐ The Spoils of War	Douglas Scott	£2.99
☐ Johnny Gurkha	E D Smith	£2.95
☐ Duel in the Dark	Peter Townsend	£3.95

Prices and other details are liable to change

ARROW BOOKS, BOOKSERVICE BY POST, PO BOX 29, DOUGLAS, ISLE OF MAN, BRITISH ISLES

NAME...

ADDRESS ....

....

....

Please enclose a cheque or postal order made out to Arrow Books Ltd. for the amount due and allow the following for postage and packing.

U.K. CUSTOMERS: Please allow 22p per book to a maximum of £3.00.

B.F.P.O. & EIRE: Please allow 22p per book to a maximum of £3.00.

OVERSEAS CUSTOMERS: Please allow 22p per book.

Whilst every effort is made to keep prices low it is sometimes necessary to increase cover prices at short notice. Arrow Books reserve the right to show new retail prices on covers which may differ from those previously advertised in the text or elsewhere.

Bestselling Fiction

☐ No Enemy But Time	Evelyn Anthony	£2.95
☐ The Lilac Bus	Maeve Binchy	£2.99
☐ Prime Time	Joan Collins	£3.50
☐ A World Apart	Marie Joseph	£3.50
☐ Erin's Child	Sheelagh Kelly	£3.99
☐ Colours Aloft	Alexander Kent	£2.99
☐ Gondar	Nicholas Luard	£4.50
☐ The Ladies of Missalonghi	Colleen McCullough	£2.50
☐ Lily Golightly	Pamela Oldfield	£3.50
☐ Talking to Strange Men	Ruth Rendell	£2.99
☐ The Veiled One	Ruth Rendell	£3.50
☐ Sarum	Edward Rutherfurd	£4.99
☐ The Heart of the Country	Fay Weldon	£2.50

Prices and other details are liable to change

ARROW BOOKS, BOOKSERVICE BY POST, PO BOX 29, DOUGLAS, ISLE
OF MAN, BRITISH ISLES

NAME...

ADDRESS...

....

....

Please enclose a cheque or postal order made out to Arrow Books Ltd. for the amount
due and allow the following for postage and packing.

U.K. CUSTOMERS: Please allow 22p per book to a maximum of £3.00.

B.F.P.O. & EIRE: Please allow 22p per book to a maximum of £3.00.

OVERSEAS CUSTOMERS: Please allow 22p per book.

Whilst every effort is made to keep prices low it is sometimes necessary to increase cover
prices at short notice. Arrow Books reserve the right to show new retail prices on covers
which may differ from those previously advertised in the text or elsewhere.